The Wo

RECONFIGURING IDENTITIES IN THE PORTUGUESE-SPEAKING WORLD

Edited by

Paulo de Medeiros and Cláudia Pazos-Alonso

VOL. 15

PETER LANG
Oxford • Bern • Berlin • Bruxelles • New York • Wien

Kristian Van Haesendonck (ed.)

The Worlds of Mia Couto

PETER LANG
Oxford • Bern • Berlin • Bruxelles • New York • Wien

Bibliographic information published by Die Deutsche Nationalbibliothek.
Die Deutsche Nationalbibliothek lists this publication in the Deutsche Nationalbibliografie; detailed bibliographic data is available on the Internet at http://dnb.d-nb.de.

A catalogue record for this book is available from the British Library.

Library of Congress Cataloging-in-Publication Data

Names: Haesendonck, Kristian van, 1974- editor.
Title: The worlds of Mia Couto / Kristian van Haesendonck [editor].
Other titles: Reconfiguring identities in the Portuguese-speaking world ; vol. 15 2235-0144.
Description: Oxford, New York : Peter Lang Ltd, 2020. | Series: Reconfiguring identities in the Portuguese-speaking world, 2235-0144 ; vol 15 | Includes bibliographical references and index. |
Identifiers: LCCN 2019048759 (print) | LCCN 2019048760 (ebook) | ISBN 9781788745949 (paperback) | ISBN 9781788745956 (ebook) | ISBN 9781788745963 (epub) | ISBN 9781788745970 (mobi)
Subjects: LCSH: Couto, Mia, 1955---Criticism and interpretation.
Classification: LCC PQ9939.C68 Z95 2020 (print) | LCC PQ9939.C68 (ebook) | DDC 869.3/42--dc23
LC record available at https://lccn.loc.gov/2019048759
LC ebook record available at https://lccn.loc.gov/2019048760

Cover image: 'Balloon – Serengeti' by Chris Parker2012. CC BY-ND 2.0.

Cover design: Peter Lang Ltd.

ISSN 2235-0144
ISBN 978-1-78874-594-9 (print) • ISBN 978-1-78874-595-6 (ePDf)
ISBN 978-1-78874-596-3 (ePub) • ISBN 978-1-78874-597-0 (mobi)

Published by Peter Lang Ltd, International Academic Publishers,
52 St Giles, Oxford, OX1 3LU, United Kingdom
oxford@peterlang.com, www.peterlang.com

Contents

Acknowledgements

The publication of this book was made possible thanks to a grant (USYRC19–22) I received from the University of Sanya. I sincerely thank the University's Board of Directors and the Dean of the School of Foreign Languages, Prof. Dr. Weimin Delcroix-Tang, for welcoming this book project and for her continuous support during the editing process.

KRISTIAN VAN HAESENDONCK

Introduction: Mia Couto, from Mozambique to the World

Mia Couto is, indisputably, one of the most important Lusophone authors nowadays. Far beyond Lusophone countries, though, his writing is appreciated in all corners of the world, and this appreciation grows with every single new publication. Although he is a very prolific and much studied writer, Mia Couto's many connections to the broader world – beyond Mozambique and the Lusophone linguistic community in which his work is usually situated and studied – have not yet been discussed.

Mia Couto is not only a master player with language, he also actively creates different worlds, while not losing touch with what we call 'reality' or, for lack of a better term, the 'real world'. This volume aims to offer a different perspective from previous scholarly work on Couto.[1] The diverse group of contributors approach Couto's work as a confluence of different literary, cultural and linguistic worlds, without shying away from its broader regional and global political and social context. *The Worlds of Mia Couto* aims to create a dialogue between a number of experts in order to lift the writer out of his linguistic and national – Mozambican – confinement, opening up the study of his work to an increasingly globalised world and the inevitable debate on World Literature. However, the contributors attempt to do so without forgetting Mia Couto's complex local and regional context: while he's firmly rooted in the African continent and African cultural traditions, we should not forget – without any prejudice – that Couto is also a writer whose *bagagem cultural* has roots in Europe, for he is deeply familiar with Europe's literary history and traditions, beyond Portuguese

1 We refer here to Grant Hamilton and David Huddart's *A Companion to Mia Couto* (Rochester, NY: James Currey, 2016), so far the only other volume of articles on Mia Couto that is available in English.

literature. Mia Couto's own rhizomic roots and literary wanderings may well make him, as Paulo de Medeiros in this volume argues, an ideal point of departure to rethink the very concept of World Literature. However, his background also exposes Couto to easy criticism for being a 'white' African author with a 'Eurocentric' heritage; most critics still reduce African literature to essentially 'black' writing, further compartmentalised into a mozaic of 'national' literatures. Another reduction happens at the heart of literary studies, which usually approaches literature under different banners: whether it is 'African', 'Mozambican', or 'Lusophone' literature, each of these labels appropriates the writer as part of its own sphere, usually ignoring the multiple connections that exist with other literatures. Mia Couto's work turns out to be a great example: it is sometimes difficult to get an overview of the different perspectives on the author's work, and the way it connects to other writings. The debate on whether his work is rather this or that kind of literature proves that we still have difficulties in the humanities in accepting that an author can be 'X and Y, and even Z', rather than the classical '*either* X *or* Y'. The institutional fossilisation of national literature departments, especially in Western European academia, is one of the key factors that still impedes truly cross-cultural and cross-literary research in the literary field. It goes without saying that Couto has primarily been studied by scholars who mostly read and write in his mother tongue, Portuguese, furthering the gap between his international readers and scholars and his Lusophone readership; in other words, he's usually seen as part of a Lusophone African tradition, locating him de facto as a member of a linguistic community he doesn't necessarily identify with, as the author himself acknowledges in the interview included at the end of this book.

Thinking about Mia Couto's 'worlds' doesn't imply that we downplay the author's local or regional coordinates, replacing them by some kind of more fashionable, 'global' perspective. It is primarily a matter of changing the centre of gravity from the national framework to an international – and explicitly comparative – one. The Mozambican context remains important, especially given its ongoing recovery process. Much of Mia Couto's diverse writing has indeed been an attempt to understand and come to terms with his country's troubled past, as well as a way to connect to other, similar traumas experienced by other African writers. Like other African countries, such as Rwanda, Angola or Burundi, today's Mozambique has slowly been recovering from the traumas it suffered during the last few decades of the twentieth century. In the sixties and early seventies, Mozambique experienced warfare and destruction during the anticolonial war which led to its independence from Portugal on 25 June 1975, following the fall of the Salazar-Caetano regime in Portugal the year before. The new government of Mozambique, led by Samora Machel, the leader of the *Frente de Libertação de Moçambique* (FRELIMO), turned the country into a one-party state. Only two years after the war of independence, a bloody civil war would hold the country in its grasp for fifteen years, claiming about one million lives. The conflict was in fact a proxy war affected by Cold War politics, opposing the Mozambican government and Mozambican National Resistance (RENAMO), a rebel group backed by South Africa and Rhodesia (now Zimbabwe). As a result of these violent wars, Mozambique sadly became known as one of the poorest countries in the world. Worse still, the country remained deeply divided, and isolated from the rest of the planet.

In spite of (recent) history being an important part of his work, Mia Couto's work is surprisingly diverse, as his newest trilogy shows, and adds up to an already impressive number of publications, ranging from poetry to non-fiction, from short-stories to historical novels. But as a writer with many hats, one should not make the mistake of reading his work only from a Mozambican national perspective. Critics have already uncovered some of the key issues in Couto's work, such as history, gender and language play, yet consistently in the author's national context. I argue that this national scope severely limits the multiplicity of transnational perspectives to which the author's work invites us (whether it is best to call these perspectives 'universal', 'international' 'global' or 'cosmopolitan', I will not discuss here). To label him a 'postmodern nationalist', as Phillip Rothwell (2004) does, is definitely to reveal an interesting tension at the heart of his work, yet it once more places the writer in an exclusively Mozambican context. Regardless of the question whether Couto is a 'postmodern' and/or a 'nationalist', or none of the above, a more productive approach would be to read Mia Couto's work from a transnational perspective to see how it connects to other literary worlds and, indeed, to what we now often refer to as 'World Literature'.

This book thus suggests it is time to move to another, transnational framework as an alternative to the way in which his work is usually studied, and also to go beyond Couto's mother tongue as the exclusive language for scholarship, which has been a further restriction on his academic reach. It is not difficult, then, to see Mia Couto's work as an embodiment of what Heidegger called 'worlding', a process of negotiation which aims to create a flexible 'assemblage' (a term Deleuze would later theorise upon)[2] of ever-renewing perceptions and realities through which we must constantly work our way to secure the world's openness: 'The work as work sets up a world. The work holds open the Open of the world'.[3] Coining the term in *Being and Time* (1927), Heidegger defined 'worlding' as a process of world making/becoming, and as such it is a determination of *Dasein*, offering measurable standards of being (both authentic and inauthentic); and worlding is also an ongoing process of the 'thinging' world. He turned the noun 'world' into an active verb, *worlding*, a productive process of world making, world becoming and 'approaching' the (empirical) world's diversity. In his own unique way, Mia Couto engages in an analogous process of 'worlding', which he adopts not only in a philosophical but in a linguistic, poetic and also – in less obvious but no less important ways – a political sense, as the essays contained in this book endeavour to show.

In 'Mia Couto and the Antinomies of World-Literature', Paulo de Medeiros explores the writer's importance in rethinking World Literature. Mia Couto's work, he argues, forces us to reflect on what the term 'World Literature' means from the margins of an increasingly globalised world, while also gauging what is lost in between discussing the local, the national

2 Deleuze defined an assemblage as a dynamic balance between heterogeneity and consistency: 'what keeps very heterogeneous elements together: e.g. a sound, a gesture, a position, etc., both natural and artificial elements. The problem is one of "consistency" or "coherence", and it is prior to the problem of behaviour. How do things take on consistency? How do they cohere? Even among very different things, an intensive continuity can be found'. Deleuze, *Two Regimes of Madness*, 179.

3 Martin Heidegger, 'The Origin of the Work of Art', in *The Continental Aesthetics Reader*, ed. Clive Cazeaux (London and New York: Routledge, 2017), 90.

and the global. As Medeiros points out, the problem with World Literature is not so much that it can be a new way of designating the 'other', but rather that it is still a way of putting certain works on a pedestal, sanctifying them as supposedly central and above other literary works. Moreover, he regrets that World Literature is trapped in a set of contradictions, such as its preference for English as a 'global language', while subscribing to a self-proclaimed universality it does not live up to. The interest of focusing on Mia Couto's work resides, furthermore, not just in his acceptance by World Literature Studies as an author producing World Literature, but also in what Medeiros calls his 'speaking for the profound humanity of the dispossessed'. Critics, he argues, should not be tempted to normalise or domesticate writers such as Couto who experiment with language, as this could be perceived as an obstacle to his inclusion in World Literature's realm. Finally, as a member of the Warwick Collective, Medeiros openly defends a materialist perspective based on World-Systems Theory, which has a focus on the periphery, a perspective Mia Couto's work is, he claims, at the vanguard of.

In 'From Nation to Imagination: Mia Couto and Language in a Comparative Perspective', David Brookshaw analyses the Mozambican author's diasporic links. He focuses on Brian Castro and Jhumpa Lahiri, two writers who have very different cultural roots yet whose work bears interesting similarities to Mia Couto's, especially when it comes to the modalities of memory Couto puts into play. However, in contrast with Castro and Lahiri, Mia Couto neither longs for nor rejects the world he grew up in. All three writers, Brookshaw argues, emphasise the diaspora of the imagination and creativity, and especially the capability of containing what he calls the 'diaspora of childhood'. The complex labyrinth of memory, and the writer's painstaking effort to reconstruct it, is also the subject of the third chapter. In 'Mia Couto and his African Context: Invention of an Origin', Ewa A. Łukaszyk traces the process of how origins are (re)invented in the writer's work. Mia Couto, she recalls, was born in the last decades of Portuguese colonialism. Łukaszyk's perspective on the writer contrasts sharply with that of Brookshaw and Medeiros, for she places his work firmly in the Mozambican context, and from there she expands on the African setting: while 'Mia Couto epitomises the native cultures of Mozambique', she argues that the attention paid by the author to the notion of kinship is more than a coincidence, as it is linked to the way he conceives of his own links to the African soil. While Medeiros sees Couto as a key figure for the reconceptualisation of World Literature, Łukaszyk emphasises the self-conscious Africanisation process at the heart of the writer's project: the African writer is a forerunner who consciously embodies – much like the character of Marianinho in Couto's novel *Um rio chamado tempo* – what she calls the emergence of a 'truly African intellectual'.

In the fourth chapter, 'Worlds of Mia Couto: The Aesthetic of the Global', Peter J. Maurits explores the connection between Couto's work and the – slippery yet inescapable – concept of globalisation. Couto's work, he argues, echoes Eric Hayot's anxiety about the 'world' and its relation to totality. The term 'world' has gained currency in literary studies over the past decades, as proven by the paradigmatic shift to World Literature; however, many questions remain unanswered. Departing from a neoliberal concept of globalisation – neoliberalism *as* globalisation – Maurits draws on key insights of what is known as the 'global aesthetic', such as narrative interlacing and homelessness, which are relevant to the Mozambican's oeuvre. Literary form, he argues, is deeply determined by globalisation, and so is film. Maurits' discussion of Couto focuses, however, on one specific work: *O Outro Pé da Sereia*, a novel whose 'globality' – the perception and representation of the world as totality – he discusses in comparison to Alejandro González Iñárritu's film *Babel*. Both the novel and film, he argues, deeply engage with a global aesthetic of homelessness and mobility, which in Couto's novel is embodied by Vila Longe, the imagined 'centre' of globalisation.

In 'Literary Ethnographies: The Idea of Nation and Writing Back in *Terra Sonâmbula* and *Macunaíma*', Kamila Krakowska Rodrigues discusses Mia Couto's novel in comparison with Mário de Andrade's best-known work. Krakowska convincingly shows that Couto's and the Brazilian writer's work invite us to engage in a dialogue with remarkable yet often forgotten, older (pre-WW1) studies from the field of ethnography, particularly two: Theodor Koch-Grünberg's *Vom Roroima zum Orinoko* and Henri Junod's classical ethnographic study *The Life of a South African Tribe*. Krakowska argues that both texts can be approached as examples of literary ethnographies, despite the fact that they are structured around their own internal logic. While *Macunaíma* is a rewriting of ethnographic works such as Grünberg's, inverting the classical format of travel writing, Couto focuses on micro-narratives, absorbing local elements from Bantu traditions and mythologies; these traditional elements are cleverly combined in *Terra Sonâmbula*, yet without any reference to specific ethnic or regional cultural differences. Likewise, Krakowska argues, Andrade's depiction of Brazil is a 'degeographised' one, blurring origins in order to enhance a non-ethnocentric concept of the Brazilian and Mozambican nations as imagined communities.

While some critics have already addressed the importance of gender issues in Couto's work, Irene Marques shows that a comparative perspective reveals interesting similarities to other – especially postcolonial – writers. In the sixth chapter, 'Female Resistance and Engagement in Combating Intersecting Powers of Colonialisms and Patriarchies in Mia Couto's *Woman of the Ashes*', Marques makes an in-depth analysis of gender issues in Couto's novel, linking it to a multiplicity of discussions regarding 'feminisms' and 'patriarchies'. Furthermore, she studies some intersections (gender, race, ethnicity) in relation to the colonial wars fought in Mozambique, where women, as elsewhere in Africa, played a key role in combating the different types of colonialism. Most accounts of heroic resistance in war, Marques argues, have a patriarchal signature and downplay or simply ignore women's contributions in the struggle against colonial domination, whereas *Woman of the Ashe*s creatively fosters an alternative, more balanced account of history.

Another way to imagine reality as 'horizontal', i.e. non-patriarchal, is through the poetic prism of the rhizome, a root metaphor which Celina Martins sees at the heart of Couto's novels, such as *A Varanda do Frangipani*. Martins interprets Mia Couto's novel as a celebration of orality, or rather a rewriting thereof, through the figure of the storyteller. The frangipani tree, she shows, is the structuring *leitmotiv* that influences the wanderings of the characters. Martins draws on the Deleuzian concept of rhizome, reappropriated by Martinican writer Edouard Glissant in his *Poetics of Relation*, to shed light on Couto's poetics of narration: each of the novel's characters narrates short stories which circulate from narrator to narrator.

The stories thus are reproduced, she argues, in several versions, yet revolve around the same necessity: the salvation of oral culture. Rhizome identity is an identity-in-becoming, based upon the opening to the Other and the *Diversité* which are to be found in multiplicity. The philosophical link to Glissant is relevant because Couto, like the Martinican, recreates the notion of rhizome as a plural identity, an urgent task in a time where cultural impurity is not only a reality but ceases to be a stigma and even becomes desirable.

In 'The Ghosts of Ngungunyane: Constructing an Ambivalent Hero', Fernanda Vilar discusses Couto's novel through a reading of the second volume of the trilogy *Sands of the Emperor* from the perspective of postmemory studies, with a special focus on the figure of Ngungunyane as a 'national ghost' who both haunts and inspires Mozambicans. Couto's novel, she argues, claims the untold ancestral experiences. The historical trauma of colonisation indeed produced narratives full of ghosts across Africa: behind official history, many stories have been silenced, and the only traces left are those which rise from the twilight zone of being and non-being, inhabited by the 'undead' – what Lacanians would refer to as the return of the untamed Real into the Symbolic order.

Finally, 'Mixing Wor(l)ds', the third section of the book, includes an interview with the author about a variety of interconnected topics, such as the relevance and role of concepts of cultural mixing (creolisation, *mestiçagem*) in a Mozambican, African and global context, with specific links to the Caribbean and Europe.

Works cited

Deleuze, Gilles. *Two Regimes of Madness: Texts and Interviews 1975–1995*. New York: Columbia University Press, 2006.

Heidegger, Martin. 'The Origin of the Work of Art.' In *The Continental Aesthetics Reader*, edited by Clive Cazeaux, 79–122. London and NY: Routledge, 2017.

Rothwell, Phillip. *A Postmodern Nationalist: Truth, Orality, and Gender in the Work of Mia Couto*. Lewisburg: Bucknell University Press, 2004.

PART I

Worlding Mia Couto

PAULO DE MEDEIROS

1 Mia Couto and the Antinomies of World-Literature

'History, meanwhile, if it is anything at all, is at one with the dialectic, and can only be the problem of which it claims to be the solution.'

– Fredric Jameson, *The Antinomies of Realism*

As the epigraph hopefully makes clear, Fredric Jameson's work *The Antinomies of Realism*[1] is in some way behind the following brief considerations on Mia Couto and World-Literature. For reading Mia Couto's works inevitably raises questions both of form and history, given his often highly experimental texts, while also always pulling readers in the direction of considering the very process of representation and its contradictory relation to material reality. In a way Mia Couto and World-Literature already constitute the first antinomy of World Literature, not only because they seem to contradict each other, but because they do not. Or, to anticipate the argument to follow, to reflect on Mia Couto and World-Literature can be a simple selective exercise destined to favour one interpretation or another of what World-Literature signifies; or it can be a completely different act of critique that simultaneously forces one to think anew what World-Literature is or can be, while, by necessity, engaging in a view of Mia Couto that sees him as neither confined to the straightjacket of the national, nor cast adrift as some sort of exotic cosmopolitan. At the beginning of a recent interview, Mia Couto, when asked about his views on World Literature as a concept, and the possibility of exoticisation, answered:

1 Fredric Jameson, *The Antinomies of Realism* (London: Verso, 2013), 24.

> *As far as I am concerned, it's a step sideways rather than a step forward. Literature, like any other art form, has always been of the world. This apparently new category is a way of classifying the literature of the so-called 'other'. But I believe that there is a process, albeit one without continuity, in which the art from Africa, Asia and South America have been acknowledged. Works from these parts of the world are beginning to gain recognition through their quality, without the need for any other additional criterion of evaluation.*[2]

The interviewers pursue the issue of World Literature a little further but what interests me is to note first of all how necessary, and almost natural, it has become to speak of Mia Couto and World Literature together, and, second, how Mia Couto, for all the, perhaps unfounded, optimism such an approach suggests, expresses a sceptical view of the concept of World Literature. If one takes a look at the development it has undergone since its coinage by Goethe, the problem with World Literature is not so much that it would be a new way of designating the 'other', but rather that it is still, as it has always been, a way of privileging and enshrining works deemed to be central and above the others, starting of course with Goethe's own. I have no intention of rehearsing here in the brief space I have the development of the concept of World Literature – something most readers probably are very familiar with.[3] Rather, what I want is to question some of the assumptions we may have concerning World Literature that become very visible when we pair Goethe and Mia Couto. Not that I want to compare the work of the two writers but rather the positions they occupy, one being very much central, the other coming more from the margins. One obvious issue will concern language and translation, as these are indeed crucial in discussions of World Literature. And, as is well known, the issue of language is also crucial in many discussions

2 Mia Couto, Grant Hamilton, and David Huddart, 'An Interview with Mia Couto', in *A Companion to Mia Couto* (Rochester, NY: James Currey, 2016), 14.

3 In the last ten years many new 'Introductions', 'Companions' and 'Readers' on World Literature have been published, some with more, others with less merit. One of the more recent, which includes a fairly broad and differentiated spectrum of perspectives, is the *Cambridge Companion to World Literature*, eds. Ben Etherington and Jarad Zimbler (Cambridge: Cambridge University Press, 2018). The use of 'World-Literature' with a hyphen reflects the practice of the Warwick Research Collective, following upon Immanuel Wallerstein's World-Systems Theory, as will be discussed further on in the text.

of Mia Couto. Translation inevitably becomes equally a concern because Portuguese, for all its claims of being one of the most spoken languages world-wide, simply cannot draw the readership of English. In the same *Companion to Mia Couto* where the interview I just quoted appears, there are two essays I would like to single out for discussion. One is by David Brookshaw, 'Mia Couto in Context', the other by Stefan Helgesson, 'Mia Couto & Translation'.[4] Helgesson's essay goes hand in hand with a previous essay of his, 'Postcolonialism and World Literature',[5] and I will refer to both. From David Brookshaw's article I want to take his reflection on how important for Mia Couto the work of Brazilian authors, specifically Guimarães Rosa, is, and how the usual uninformed claims in the press about his magical realism must be set aside. The contextualisation of Mia Couto is essential for any understanding of how his work both enhances and alters World-Literature, and this is something David Brookshaw already proposes in his essay.

I want to start addressing the issue more directly, by looking at the question of translation. Helgesson's writing is always very clear and well-informed and usually lays out a whole sketch of a number of intellectual debates. In 'Mia Couto & Translation' his point of departure is the complementary and somewhat opposed views on the role of translation enunciated by David Damrosch and Emily Apter; namely, Damrosch's assertion that works of world literature gain in translation and Apter's view that there are some works of literature that simply cannot be translated.[6] Granted, this is a crude oversimplification but could be effective in getting a discussion on Mia Couto and World Literature started. As I have had a chance of arguing elsewhere,[7] I cannot subscribe to Damrosch's view, either in its

4 David Brookshaw, 'Mia Couto in Context', in *A Companion to Mia Couto*, 17–24. Stefan Helgesson, 'Mia Couto & Translation', in *A Companion to Mia Couto*, 140–156.

5 Stefan Helgesson, 'Postcolonialism and World Literature: Rethinking the Boundaries', *Interventions: A Journal of Postcolonial Studies* 16.4 (2014): 483–500.

6 David Damrosch, *What Is World Literature?* (Princeton: Princeton University Press, 2003). Emily Apter, *Against World Literature: On the Politics of Untranslatibility* (London: Verso, 2013).

7 Paulo de Medeiros, 'Translation and Cosmopolitanism', in *Translation and World Literature*, ed. Susan Bassnett (London and New York: Routledge, 2019), 60–74.

absolute vagueness, or in what it implies. Clearly translation is very important and sometimes even essential. Mia Couto's world renown would not be the same were his works not translated into about twenty languages. Yet, had his works remained untranslated, they would not have lost any of their significance and would still be a part of World Literature as a system. In terms of circulation, the numbers of sales would have been much reduced but the works would still have had a global reach. However, this is not quite the point I would like to make. Stefan Helgesson focuses on the variety of translations (this is something he had already sketched out in 'Postcolonialism and World Literature'), and even though he does acknowledge the importance of the English translation, for obvious reasons he would like to claim significance for other, less central, languages, including his own, Swedish. In principle that is a move that I find appropriate – yet I cannot but disagree with the view he puts forth of a 'normalising' or even 'domesticating' of Mia Couto's radical language experimentation when he refers to the English translation. Without engaging any further with this argument, I would rather draw on the fact that language experimentation, although an important feature of the writing of Mia Couto, cannot be seen as its defining essence to the detriment of all other achievements. More to the point even, language experimentation could have been perceived as an obstacle to the inclusion of Mia Couto within World Literature. One could think that his language games not only pose a linguistic challenge but also are too much of a marker of national and cultural identification. The opposite, I would like to suggest, is true. Obviously the language games are going to be always culture and language specific but they should not be misunderstood as national. Since Helgesson in both essays mentions one very specific and small example, I would like to refer to it here: the question turns on the neologism, 'pertubabado', which we find in a statement by Kindzu in *Terra Sonâmbula* (*Sleepwalking Land*).[8] Helgesson notes: 'In the English translation the full sentence reads: "I went in, perturbed, aflame with intention" (Couto 2006: 96); in Swedish: "Omtumlad trädde jag in till henne, blygförvirrad och brinnande av hemliga avsikter" (Couto

8 Mia Couto, *Terra Sonâmbula* (Lisbon: Caminho, 1992). *Sleepwalking Land*, trans. David Brookshaw (London: Serpent's Tail, 2006).

1995: 109); in Portuguese: "Entrei, perturbabado, ardendo de intenção" (Couto 2009a: 140)'.[9] Helgesson's own understating of the effects of Mia Couto's creation are imaginative even if somewhat baffling: 'The redundant syllable "ba" – which has recurred in all ten Portuguese editions of *Terra* to date, so it is not a typo – creates an auditory, stammering effect in Portuguese, as though the first-person narrator had pronounced the word in a perturbed state of mind.'[10] I wonder what happened to what I think will be the most obvious meaning to Portuguese speakers, of 'drooled' (babado). This sort of misreading – perhaps a happy misreading – is inevitable and already points to the need for questioning the role of the translator rather than assuming that a recreation of word games is essential.

Very briefly, as a way of drawing the main point on the issue of translation: precisely because the language of Mia Couto is so full of such word games, it could have been an obstacle to his incorporation into World Literature. That the opposite is true indicates that linguistic complexity, and the relative obscurity of a semi-peripheral language such as Portuguese in terms of the global market, are no impediment. This had also been remarked upon by Helgesson who rightly notes that 'translation can never be just one thing in relation to Couto's work, but will exhibit a wide repertoire of solutions as well as contradictions. As such, Couto provides an illuminating case study in World Literature ...'.[11] I agree, but for somewhat different reasons, as I think that Mia Couto's work not only fits in with World Literature, no matter what definition one would invoke, but questions and exposes some of its inner contradictions and blind spots.

From a brief reflection on the apparent contradiction concerning Mia Couto's highly particular use of language and his entry into World Literature, I would like to move to a consideration of another seemingly discordant contradiction between the national and the global. There can be no doubt that Mia Couto's perspective is a Mozambican one and that he often, if not always, is concerned with Mozambican concerns. This is not to say that he speaks for Mozambique in any way. The wish to reduce a writer to a national identity is common to many readers and critics, and

9 Stefan Helgesson, 'Postcolonialism and World Literature', 490.

10 Ibid., 490.

11 Stefan Helgesson, 'Mia Couto & Translation', 141.

Mia Couto is certainly not alone in refuting such facile identifications. Even if one were to go beyond such banalities and consider the polemical claim once argued by Fredric Jameson that all 'third-world' literature is a national allegory, one would have to immediately qualify that.[12] Jameson's formulation was perhaps crude, unnecessarily provocative, and sweeping; yet, with the benefit of time, there is also much in it that cannot be denied. One reason might well be that to a great extent rising literatures in many parts of the world were indeed deeply engaged in creating images of the nation. If one looks to a concrete example, already mentioned, *Sleepwalking Land*, one can see how there is much in Jameson's claim that could be made to fit that novel as its reflection on the devastation of the civil war in many ways is presented in an allegorical mode. That Mia Couto's method does not avoid some inner contradictions has already been seized upon by Phillip Rothwell, in his discussion of Mia Couto as a 'postmodern nationalist'.[13] However – and this is what I find more salient – the novel is at the same time a powerful call for a radically different notion of belonging that would transcend the nation. If anything, as most readers would agree, it is the Indian Ocean which is presented as the proper space for identification. As Bill Ashcroft notes, '[t]he sea is a fascinating postcolonial space, because it completely transcends the idea of the bounded nation'.[14] As such, belonging would always be a transnational category that does not ignore the nation

12 Fredric Jameson, 'Third-World Literature in the Era of Multinational Capitalism', *Social Text* 15 (1986): 65–88. The most extensive and lucid discussion of the controversy generated by this essay and its pitfalls that dispels the many misreadings that accrued around it was published by Neil Lazarus as the second chapter to his *The Postcolonial Unconscious* (Cambridge: Cambridge University Press, 2011), 85–113. However, see also Fredric Jameson's own recent take on the controversy, in which he goes much further than arguing in the defence of his initial position, instead offering a new reflection on the meaning, and (political) use, of the notion of allegory: Fredric Jameson, 'Political: National Allegory: Commentary', in *Allegory and Ideology* (London: Verso, 2019), 187–216.

13 Phillip Rothwell, *A Postmodern Nationalist: Truth, Orality, and Gender in the Work of Mia Couto* (Lewisburg: Bucknell University Press, 2004).

14 Bill Ashcroft, 'The Multiple Worlds of Mia Couto', in *A Companion to Mia Couto*, eds. Grant Hamilton and David Huddart (Rochester, NY: James Currey, 2016), 112.

but refuses to grant it any primacy when imagining a possible future free from the devastation brought about by war.

One of the defining characteristics of Mia Couto's works, and one he has consistently drawn attention to, is hybridity. Within postcolonial studies the notion of hybridity has long been established as a key concept, following the work of Homi Bhabha.[15] In as much as Mia Couto reflects on the fusion of cultures and languages in Mozambique, in Africa and in the world, there is somewhat of a convergence between his views and those expressed by Bhabha. However, personally, I find the way in which Mia Couto expounds hybridity to be differently grounded, and to draw on the actual lives of people, instead of being something abstract and for the most part just celebratory. Mia Couto defends the importance of hybridity, even to the point of, rightly, asserting that the notion of purity simply does not apply to human beings and that all of our actions are based

15 The most relevant reference here is Homi K. Bhaba's *The Location of Culture*, initially published in 1994 and reissued in 2004 (London: Routledge). See especially Chapter 6, 'Signs Taken for Wonders: Questions of Ambivalence and Authority under a Tree outside Delhi, May 1817', 145–174; and Chapter 8, 'DissemiNation: Time, Narrative, and the Margins of the Modern Nation', 199–244. As influential as Bhabha's notion of hybridity has been in postcolonial studies, it remains problematic, as I see it, for even as it attempts to provide a way of counteracting the ills of colonialism, it still can be seen as too simply engaging in complex abstractions at a remove from social and historical reality. In this sense, the most lucid critique has been provided, arguably, by Neil Lazarus in *The Postcolonial Unconscious* (Cambridge, Cambridge University Press, 2001). Lazarus, rightly, in my view, takes mainstream postcolonial discourse to task, for its evading of social and political specificities in its often blind assumptions: 'Among these assumptions and investments, I would list in particular the following: a constitutive anti-Marxism; an undifferentiating disavowal of all forms of nationalism and a corresponding exaltation of migrancy, liminality, hybridity, and multiculturality; an hostility towards "holistic forms of social explanation" (towards totality and systemic analysis); an aversion to dialectics; and a refusal of an antagonistic or struggle-based model of politics', p. 21. With specific respect to the Lusophone situation and its specific issues concerning racial policies during the Salazar regime and the thorny questions of 'Lusotropicalism' and 'Lusophony', see Ana Paula Ferreira's 'Contesting Miscegenation and Lusotropicalism: Women and the Portuguese Colonial Order', in *Itinerâncias: Percursos e representações da pós-colonialidade*, eds. Elena Brugioni et al., Braga: Húmus, 2012, 101–120.

on exchanges. And this is a point on which perhaps the work of Mia Couto could be invoked as providing a corrective for what sometimes appears as a light-headed intellectual abstraction that ends up reifying that which it would like to praise. The same can be seen, I would like to suggest, with regards to World Literature and I hope to address that directly by focusing on two issues: first, that the current debates on World Literature, indeed, much of its strength as a field of study, come from the impact that postcolonial studies have had, as well as on their announced death; second, that the reconceptualisation of World Literature achieved by the Warwick Research Collective in their programmatic volume, *Combined and Uneven Development*, with its focus on World-Systems Theory, can offer a materialist perspective attuned to the periphery that would be more consistent with the challenges posed by Mia Couto.[16]

In 'Postcolonialism and World Literature', Stefan Helgesson goes straight to the core of the first issue and his choice of authors to help with the theoretical reflections, Mia Couto and Assia Djebar, is apt, even if Mia Couto really is made to bear much of the argument. His main contention is clear and lucid: 'given the tensions between their subjective position and the transnational valency of literature, writers from colonies and postcolonies are of specific and paradigmatic importance to the theorisation of world literature'.[17] There are many points in which I agree with Helgesson, and find his capacity to synthesise debates and his wide reading very helpful. I also want to note that if he stays fairly close to the dominating voices in the World Literature pantheon – Pascale Casanova, Franco Moretti, besides the ubiquitous David Damrosch and Emily Apter – when it comes to postcolonial studies he also draws, without necessarily endorsing it, on the left wing of the field, represented by Neil Lazarus and Rob Nixon. His choice of Mia Couto is significant even if the comparison with Djebar remains too superficial and is, arguably, conceptually flawed, given the fact that even if both can be claimed as African, Djebar had long been accepted, even if not always smoothly, into the centre of French letters as a member of the Académie Française. In comparison, Mia Couto, with all

16 Warwick Research Collective. *Combined and Uneven Development: Towards a New Theory of World-Literature* (Liverpool: Liverpool University Press, 2015).

17 Stefan Helgesson, 'Postcolonialism and World Literature', 483, 490.

of his prizes and world-wide recognition, can be said to remain a much more peripheral figure. And there would be other reasons to wish for a different comparison, with the work of a Coetzee for instance, but that is another discussion altogether. What I want to focus on is the choice of Mia Couto to illustrate the relationship between postcolonial studies and World Literature.

This troubled relationship reflects the malaise expressed by many of the most prolific postcolonial critics, notably in an MLA forum in 2007.[18] A strong dissenting voice, but a fairly isolated one it seems, was that of Robert J. C. Young in an article published five years later with the title of 'Postcolonial Remains'.[19] Without revisiting that debate, I want to seize on the way in which it seems, to me at least, as if postcolonial studies, having passed through the rites of entry into the groves of academia and having become a very successful field throughout the majority of English-speaking universities, then lost its lustre and was no longer appealing, with ecocriticism, the posthuman, and, indeed World Literature, beckoning as hot new fields capable of attracting vigorous discussions and, significantly, offering better prospects for employment. Without denying the reality of the academic enterprise and its less scholarly attributes, I still find it cynical to treat a field of studies as if it were no more than a designer label with a limited shelf life. Helgesson is exactly right as he makes the link between postcolonial studies, World Literature and Mia Couto. As Helgesson clearly notes, 'if postcolonialism has drawn on the energies of anticolonial nationalism, the civil rights movement in the United States, and 'third-worldist' activism in Europe, which all spoke to the urgent need for social justice, World Literature studies today emerges at a moment when clearly hierarchical new superpowers – such as India and China – with an investment in classicist literary heritages have risen to prominence. Can these trajectories be combined? Not always'[20]. But the article, for all its suggestiveness, lacks a compelling way out of what it does not even posit as a contradiction. Mia

18 'Editor's Column: The End of Postcolonial Theory? A Roundtable with Sunil Agnani, Fernando Coronil, Gaurav Desai, Mamadou Diouf, Simon Gikandi, Susie Tharu, and Jennifer Wenzel', *PMLA* 122, no. 3 (2007): 633–51.

19 Robert J. C. Young. 'Postcolonial Remains', *New Literary History*, 2012, 43: 19–42.

20 Stefan Helgesson, 'Postcolonialism and World Literature', 484.

Couto, conversely, even if perhaps he had no such intention, is pointing to the contradiction when he states that in his view World Literature is but a euphemism for 'other', that is, less than central, literature. To many, myself included, postcolonial critique was not simply yet another mode of criticism but an important analytical tool to expose the imbalances of power and asymmetries inherent in the modern world as a consequence of imperial and colonial aggression and, as some would also add, the rise of capitalism as a dominant system. The adaptation of postcolonial perspectives from the Anglophone world where they initially developed to other spheres, such as the Francophone and the Lusophone, implied not just an adaptation of concepts to suit different contextual specificities, but actually a reconceptualisation of the field itself. Seen from a World-Systems Theory perspective, Portugal's semi-peripheral position – as Boaventura de Sousa Santos also argued[21] – actually gave rise to a form of invisibility, even a double invisibility, for the postcolonial works written in Portuguese. In a sense, only a handful of writers has been able to breach that. In the case of Portugal, José Saramago, with the Nobel prize, has managed to do so, and perhaps Lobo Antunes as well, but more partially. In the case of Lusophone Africa, Mia Couto represents a unique case, with perhaps José Eduardo Agualusa coming afterwards.

World-Literature as traditionally conceived of as a canon or a Republic of Letters, or even a mode of reading, cannot escape the contradiction between its avowed universality and its much more limited focus on a concentration of writers from a handful of countries, with English clearly dominating as the global language. Sticking to such a view of World Literature would in the end actually serve to reinforce a Western norm with newer works being admitted to the select group but having to prove themselves and, perhaps, perpetually remaining on a different footing. That is one way in which I would understand Mia Couto's view of World Literature as a step sideways, a detour that might eventually take us forward, but remains a detour. However, if one takes a view of World Literature based on Wallerstein's notion of it as an interaction between centre and

21 See for instance, his seminal, even if by now in many ways superseded, essay: Boaventura de Sousa Santos. 'Between Prospero and Caliban: Colonialism, Postcolonialism, and Inter-Identity.' *Luso-Brazilian Review* 39, no. 2 (2002): 9–43.

periphery – with a significant role played by the semi-periphery as a hybrid place that is both centre and periphery depending on whether it interacts with its own periphery or its own centre – then one could see that what Mia Couto does, and represents, is very much part of a peripheral or semi-peripheral move to contest the notion of a hegemonic centre.

In other words, in such a perspective it is precisely writing such as that of Mia Couto's that can best expose the antinomies of World Literature and call for its renewal from the margins. In the conclusion of 'What Africa Does the African Writer Write About?', his speech at the award ceremony for the Prize for the Twelve Best African Novels in Cape Town in 2012, Mia Couto calls for a future in which '[w]e want and dream of a nation and a continent that no longer needs heroes'.[22] While these words have a specific context and a clear historical referent in armed struggle against varied forms of colonialism and imperialism, they also could be taken as a way of calling for an understanding of literature – Mozambican, African, World Literature – that would break through the hegemonic controls – the printing, distribution and reception networks including prizes, festivals and awards – that still work in favour of the erstwhile imperialists.

Obviously one could say that the propulsion of Mia Couto to the status of cultural hero is yet another way of exoticising him and attempting to co-opt his transgressive potential. Perhaps, but in many ways Mia Couto's work is but the opening of a different conception of World Literature, one that does not merely embellish an institutionalised postcolonial critique with the promise of the global, but rather one in which its evolving contradictions can continue to be problematised and developed. When Jameson claims that, '[h]istory, meanwhile, if it is anything at all, is at one with the dialectic, and can only be the problem of which it claims to be the solution',[23] one way of understanding this claim is to look at antinomies as always central and constitutive of any kind of discourse. At the same time it is also a way of avoiding being blinded by the promise of solutions which might, in turn, merely be themselves the problem they would resolve.

22 Mia Couto, 'What Africa Does the African Writer Write About?', in *Pensativities: Essays & Provocations*, ed. David Brookshaw (Windsor, Ontario: Biblioasis, 2015), 27.

23 Fredric Jameson, *The Antinomies of Realism* (London: Verso, 2013), 6.

World-Literature if taken on the rarefied abstract level that has characterised much of the debate risks being nothing more than an aesthetic game for a minority that dreams itself cosmopolitan, free from the still sticky demands of a postcolonial critique that was, in the lesson of Edward Said, always of the world and that sought to redress gross systemic inequality. The promise, to me, of Mia Couto as World-Literature, then, is not so much his conveniently being received by the literary and critical centre, but rather his unabated speaking for the profound humanity of the dispossessed.

A consideration of Mia Couto in a World-Literature paradigm must contemplate two issues: on the one hand, the troubled relationship between Africa and World-Literature, and on the other, the dangers involved in identifying Mia Couto with the idea of the Mozambican nation, as I already suggested. Or, to put it in a slightly different way, how does a discussion of the work of Mia Couto contribute to a problematisation, and possibly even a change, in the still prevalent dismissal of most African literatures from World-Literature? And, especially given Mia Couto's often expressed distrust of the nation as a concept, but also given the never ceasing questioning of his authenticity as an 'African' writer, given that, born to Portuguese parents, he is white, the tendency to read him as standing in for Mozambique is as myopic as it is tempting.

Although a full consideration of the relationship between African literatures and World-Literature is clearly outside the scope of any single article, it is perhaps the very first point that needs to be addressed, albeit in concise form. First of all, there is the issue of the still prevalent neglect of African literatures in most discussions of world literature. There are exceptions of course: think of a Chinua Achebe, a J. M. Coetzee, or a Chimamanda Ngozi Adichie. But even if some, almost exclusively Anglophone, occasionally Francophone, works by African authors have become established within the canon of great authors, then usually it is always as representatives of one or another form of alterity, always already inscribed in the very designation of 'African' as traditionally conceived by Western critics. In that sense, Mia Couto's suspicion of the designation World Literature is clearly warranted. There are a few attempts that try to break out of this, even if tentatively. For instance, a recent issue of the *Journal of World Literature*, guest-edited by Francesca Orsini and Laetitia

Zecchini, specifically tries to start addressing the problem of exclusion by focusing on *The Locations of (World) Literature: Perspectives from Africa and South Asia*.[24] As a beginning, it is laudable, even if necessarily limited and prone to mix categories and issues as well as continents. Surely, there are aspects in common to the literatures of Asia and Africa in relation to the canonical Western view of World Literature, but then much the same could be said about South America, the incorporation and co-optation of the writers of the so-called boom notwithstanding, and this is simply left out altogether. Thus, even though I would agree with the principle behind moving towards a more concerted consideration of both African and Asian literatures in the sphere of World Literature, I would expect that some attention might have been paid to Lusophone writers, given that more often than not they suffer from redoubled forms of invisibility.

It is not so much that any journal issue perforce will be restricted, or that any kind of start to address a problem is already a solution, or even that the editors might be entitled to make their own choices of whom they would like to put forward for admittance at the high table of World Literature. Methodologically too, there is a shunning of systematicity in favour of the aleatory that I find troubling. This can be seen for instance in the light way in which the editors briefly and summarily dismiss World Literature perspectives based on a world-systems theory in their introduction. They start by asserting, while citing David Damrosch, the importance of considering that every perspective is based on a specific positioning and then proceed to offer their own opinion, though without in any way grounding it: 'Yet in world-system or field theories, and in approaches that focus on 'global' circulation, this important insight gets sidelined or forgotten. Applied to literature, world-system and field theories produce a limited range of possible and alternative positions, as if dealing the players a very small pack of cards: subjection or revolt, emulation or appropriation, marginality or cosmopolitanism, indigeneity or foreignness'.[25] The problem is not with

24 *Journal of World Literature* 4 (2019).

25 Francesca Orsini and Laetitia Zecchini, 'The Locations of (World) Literature: Perspectives from Africa and South Asia.' *Journal of World Literature* 4 (2019): 1–2. The lack of any grounding or reference might appear puzzling. However, readers might remember that in an earlier piece, 'Significant

recognising that any and all perspectives always are grounded somewhere in space and time – I will leave aside the issue of what appears to be a misreading of World-Systems Theory[26] – nor with the fact that perspectives often are multiple, complex, and even contradictory. The problem, as I see it, lies more with the inability to see that, though methodologically and ideologically radically different from each other, there is a mutual goal to both sides, the desire to break up a more traditional and conventional notion of World Literature.

Thinking about Mia Couto in particular, this problem is particularly distressing, even if perhaps not totally unexpected. There can be no doubt that Mozambique, as the ground for Mia Couto's narrative, is indispensable and irreplaceable. At the same time, attempts to combine this realisation with traditional, static, notions of the nation, territory, language and identity can only backfire. At this point one really should question not only what is the relationship of Africa to World Literature but also what is the positioning of an African writer in that constellation. If Africa still tends to be elided from discussions of World Literature, the solution is not to try to make this or that great writer fit into such an exclusionary and exclusivist view of World Literature. Rather, one should be asking how

Geographies: In Lieu of World Literature', Francesca Orsini, with Karima Laachir, and Sara Marzagora, had already taken more systematic approaches to World Literature to task, and especially the work of the Warwick Research Collective, for being somehow reductive. There is a clear ideological rift between such a position and the materialist one advocated by the Warwick Research Collective that cannot be breached. In this earlier piece, there was at least an attempt at naming the fissure and provide a reference so readers could go and inform themselves. The latter article somehow, dispenses with all of that and as such lacks even the directness evident in the earlier article. The subtitle of that one, 'In Lieu of World Literature', clearly conveyed the notion of replacing World Literature altogether with something else ('Significant Geographies'), whereas the more recent one, by aligning itself with David Damrosch's pronouncements on World Literature, creates the appearance of still wanting to have something to say about the field.

26 The misreading of the work done by the Warwick Research Collective in *Combined and Uneven Development* seems especially puzzling, considering that two full chapters are devoted to African writers, Tayeb Salih from Sudan, and Ivan Vladislavic from South Africa, besides the general discussion of the importance of the periphery.

African writers must necessarily change such a view. As a Mozambican writer Mia Couto could be labelled a peripheral writer, from a continent that many still would prefer to ignore or wrongly perceive as not having fully embraced modernity. Yet, in reality, Africa is not the assemblage of clichés many in the West would like to uphold, nor is Mia Couto an ignored writer. If anything, the danger here is for us once more to start wanting to identify him too closely with the nation, holding him up, as it were, to serve as representing Mozambique. Clearly, his international acclaim can be said inadvertently to create some of that. Nonetheless, one should bear in mind always that contemporary Mozambican literature is rich, and other writers, with markedly different writing strategies and aims, such as Paulina Chiziane, Ungulani Ba Ka Khosa and João Paulo Borges Coelho, to name a few, also have a very significant literary career and it would not make sense to speak of Mozambican literature without considering their varied contributions.

Mia Couto has often reflected on the relationships between literature and society and specifically between literature and the nation and has, I would argue, always tried to find ways to resist the exoticising that still seems to go hand in hand with any form of recognition by a Western-centred and dominated literary system. Of course none of this is individually specific to Mia Couto. J. M. Coetzee succeeded in exposing many of the antinomies I have been exploring so far in his chapter of the novel *Elizabeth Costello*, under the title 'The Novel in Africa'.[27] In that fictional account of two writers turned entertainers aboard a luxury liner, one Australian, the other South African, one a white woman, the other a black man, Coetzee provides a mordant critique of the very process by which writers so easily become co-opted by the triple mirage of nation, race, and, language. In many ways, throughout his oeuvre, Mia Couto also has never ceased to critique received notions of what Mozambique is and what his role as a Mozambican writer might be in terms of not just aesthetic, but socio-political responsibilities as well. It is in this sense, and not on the old terms of a conventional

27 J. M. Coetzee. 'The Novel in Africa' in *Elizabeth Costello* (London: Vintage, 1999), 35–58.

World Literature thirsty for prizes and best-seller figures, I would argue, that one should read Mia Couto as part of World-Literature.

The view of World-Literature 'as the literature of the world-system – of the modern capitalist world-system, that is', put forward by the Warwick Research Collective, is unabashedly materialist and dispenses with the category of 'genius' altogether, besides many other would-be existentialist or pseudo-phenomenological flirtations with the concept. It does not, however, privilege the West as the defining cradle of modernity. Indeed, at the very core of a conceptualisation of World-Literature in terms of combined and uneven development, is the notion that capitalism, in its inexorable conquest of new markets and search for more resources to explore will always cut across national and other 'geographical' divides. Furthermore, such a view of World-Literature rejects notions of belatedness or alternate modernities. Key to this line of thought is the work of Fredric Jameson, especially his *A Singular Modernity*. As the Warwick Research Collective puts it,

> Jameson speaks then of the singularity of modernity, of modernity as a globally dispersed general 'situation'. 'Modernity' does not mark the relationship between some formations (that are 'modern') and others (that are not 'modern', or not yet so). So it is not a matter of pitting France against Mali, say, or New York City against Elk City, Oklahoma. Uneven development is not a characteristic of 'backward' formations only. Middlesbrough and North East Lincolnshire are in the United Kingdom as well as London and the Home Counties – and London itself, of course, is among the more radically unevenly developed cities in the world.[28]

Among other advantages, as I see it, this approach can be said to reject any facile dichotomies between core and periphery, or between the 'West and the Rest'. To avoid any possible confusion: I am in no way advocating any conflation of either historical or cultural specificities. Far from it, what this view proposes is a radical refusal of any notion, vague or otherwise, of Western primacy or superiority. If anything, by focusing on the importance of the periphery to understand the advancement of World-Literature, what this view could be said effectively to promote is a different way to include African literature, not so much as an addition, belated or otherwise, to the universe of World-Literature, but rather as one of its driving forces.

28 Warwick Research Collective. *Combined and Uneven Development*, 12.

So, even if one should respect Mia Couto's suspicion that attempts to subsume African literatures, including his own work, under the label of World Literature, one should also recognise that what the conceptualisation of World-Literature in the terms of the Warwick Research Collective, does, is call precisely for a recognition of the transformative potential of African Literatures, and certainly of the work of Mia Couto.

Before concluding, I would like still to refer to one issue that seems to me to be crucial and that would require much more consideration. At the same time that we should be comparing Mia Couto to other writers, such as Assia Djebar or J. M. Coetzee, we should also not forget to read him in comparison to other writers who work in Portuguese, from João Guimarães Rosa, whom Mia Couto acknowledges as having been personally of great influence, to many others. Obviously, as two former Portuguese colonies, both Brazil and Mozambique will have a certain number of affinities that are rooted not only in a common history of oppression but also in shared cultural norms, since Brazil's economic success was for centuries dependent on the importation of African slaves. And this obviously, is not limited to Brazil and Mozambique but involves all of the countries once dominated by Portugal, which, after independence, continued using and developing the Portuguese language. Again, to avoid any possible confusion: I am not advocating any form of exalted relationship between these various nations and their literatures, as often is the case whenever the vague notion of *Lusofonia* is invoked; far from it.[29] However, I think that one of the ways in which the work of Mia Couto, among other writers who use Portuguese, can serve to change a more conventional view of World Literature, lies precisely in the fact that these countries already constitute a system among themselves, and that their literatures, even if they appear individual and unconnected, already interact in ways that make them part of a system that calls for more study.

Mia Couto – even if not alone of course – occupies a pivotal role in the process of reshaping World-Literature from the periphery, for he

29 The polemics surrounding *Lusofonia* seem to be constantly rekindled and it is not my intention to engage with them at all; especially as I have had occasion to argue my views (on its pitfalls) at some length. See Paulo de Medeiros, 'Lusophony or the Haunted Logic of Postempire', *Lusotopie* 17 (2018): 227–247.

embodies a borderland consciousness that, I think, is key for the kind of World-Literature I have in mind.[30] He himself is very much aware of always having occupied a series of liminal spaces, as he candidly notes:

> My country contains within it various countries, profoundly divided among a wide variety of social and cultural universes. I am Mozambican, the son of Portuguese immigrants, I lived under the colonial system, I fought for independence, I lived through radical social change from socialism to capitalism, from the revolution to civil war. I was born in a pivotal period, between a world that was being born and another that was dying: between a country that never was and another that is still being born. This situation of living on a frontier left its mark on me.[31]

How far we are from purely celebratory versions of hybridity for easy consumption in the West, as Mia Couto grounds his liminal experience on the violence of major socio-political upheavals. To conclude, I would like to refer back to the epigraph taken from Fredric Jameson and suggest that Mia Couto's works, as well as his life, do present us with a continuous series of apparently contradictory situations; and to point out that history, the history of Mozambique as he has lived it, is one that does appear indeed to be both problem and solution, to be the problem for which it seems to proffer a solution. What Jameson refers to as a dialectical relationship, and which Mia Couto, judging from comments like the one just cited, might refer to as being on the frontier, are, I would suggest,

30 This too would need more reflection than I can do in the present context. A place to start might be the comments on Tayeb Salih's, *Season of Migration to the North* (London: Heinemann, 1969) by the Warwick Research Collective: 'On the assumption that the novel's cognitive and aesthetic dimensions are inseparable, we will attempt to retrieve its historically located substance and social and political registers from both "story" and stylistics. But it seems to us that any attempt at a realist reading will be frustrated by a narrative that openly accommodates transgressions of credibility and is hospitable to the phantasmagoric' (*Combined and Uneven Development*, 83). This discussion immediately then refers to the work of Michael Löwy and his notion of "irrealism", a concept that would be much more fruitful to apply to the work of Mia Couto than the misleading (and misnamed) 'magical realism'. See Michael Löwy, 'L'Irréalisme Critique', *Actuel Marx* 45 (2009): 52–65.

31 Mia Couto, 'The Brazilian Sertão in the Mozambican Savannah', in *Pensativities: Essays and Provocations*, trans. David Brookshaw (Windsor, Ontario: Biblioasis, 2015), 50.

similar inasmuch as they reflect the very conditions of society that the literary text both registers and seeks to shape. And although some might find my reading of Mia Couto to be lopsided in its insistence on a political significance for World-Literature, I would maintain that Mia Couto, even if rightly rejecting any reductive instrumentalisation or co-opting of literature by the political, never ceases to reflect on, and expose, the political nature of culture and a writer's duty to bear witness and to imagine a different, better world. Talking about the way in which language becomes perverted so as to hide reality while pretending it has been changed, Mia Couto came very close actually to Jameson's terms, when he said that 'Many institutions that ought to be producing ideas are now producing reports (…). Instead of solutions, problems are found'.[32] As much as Mia Couto is a writer deeply concerned with the past, with memory (and forgetting), he also is keenly aware of the way in which the past often is not really past. As he notes in another of his essays, 'Colonialism didn't die when countries became independent. There was a change of shift and of crew. Present-day colonialism has dispensed with colonials and has become indigenised within our territories.'[33] Just as Mia Couto alerts us to the insidiousness inherent in the perpetuation of structures of colonial oppression – closely linked obviously to capitalism, as he made evident several times in a speech he gave to the Association of Mozambican Economists, in Maputo on August 2003 – so we could also pay attention to the insidiousness through which older forms of privileging certain kinds of literature adapt by incorporating, usually with great fanfare, newer elements. If one is serious about a renewed form of understanding World-Literature, one that does not simply condescend to accept writers like Mia Couto into its fold so as to better preserve its forms of privilege, then one should rather think of Mia Couto and other writers like him, as heralding the future of World-Literature, not in spite of, but precisely because of, their peripheral, liminal, and ever-shifting positions.

32 Mia Couto, 'The Seven Dirty Shoes', in *Pensativities: Essays and Provocations*, 103.

33 Mia Couto, 'The Frontier of Culture', in *Pensativities: Essays and Provocations*, 3.

Works cited

Apter, Emily. *Against World Literature: On the Politics of Untranslatibility*. London: Verso, 2013.

Ashcroft, Bill. 'The Multiple Worlds of Mia Couto'. In *A Companion to Mia Couto*, edited by Grant Hamilton and David Huddart, 106–124. Rochester, NY: James Currey, 2016.

Bhaba. Homi K. *The Location of Culture*. London: Routledge, 2004.

Brookshaw, David. 'Mia Couto in Context'. In *A Companion to Mia Couto*, edited by Grant Hamilton and David Huddart, 17–24. Rochester, NY: James Currey, 2016.

Coetzee, J. M. 'The Novel in Africa'. In J. M. Coetzee, *Elizabeth Costello*, 35–58. London: Vintage, 1999.

Couto, Mia, Grant Hamilton, and David Huddart. 'An Interview with Mia Couto', translated by David Brookshaw. In *A Companion to Mia Couto*, edited by Grant Hamilton and David Huddart, 14–16. Rochester, NY: James Currey, 2016.

Couto, Mia. *Pensativities: Essays and Provocations*. Translated by David Brookshaw. Windsor, Ontario: Biblioasis, 2015.

Couto, Mia. *Terra Sonâmbula* (Lisbon: Caminho, 1992). *Sleepwalking Land*, translated by David Brookshaw. London: Serpent's Tail, 2006.

Damrosch, David. *What Is World Literature?* Princeton: Princeton University Press, 2003.

de Medeiros, Paulo. 'Lusophony or the Haunted Logic of Postempire'. *Lusotopie* 17 (2018): 227–247.

de Medeiros, Paulo. 'Translation and Cosmopolitanism.' In *Translation and World Literature*, edited by Susan Bassnett, 60–74. London and New York: Routledge, 2019.

'Editor's Column: The End of Postcolonial Theory? A Roundtable with Sunil Agnani, Fernando Coronil, Gaurav Desai, Mamadou Diouf, Simon Gikandi, Susie Tharu, and Jennifer Wenzel.' *PMLA* 122, no. 3 (2007): 633–51.

Etherington, Ben and Jarad Zimbler, eds. *Cambridge Companion to World Literature*. Cambridge: Cambridge University Press, 2018.

Ferreira, Ana Paula. 'Contesting Miscegenation and Lusotropicalism: Women and the Portuguese Colonial Order'. In *Itinerâncias: Percursos e representações da Pós-colonialidade*, edited by Elena Brugioni, Joana Passos, Andrea Sarabando, and Marie-Manuelle Silva, 101–120. Braga: Húmus, 2012.

Helgesson, Stefan. 'Mia Couto & Translation'. In *A Companion to Mia Couto*, edited by Grant Hamilton and David Huddart, 140–156. Rochester, NY: James Currey, 2016.

Helgesson, Stefan. 'Postcolonialism and World Literature: Rethinking the Boundaries'. *Interventions: A Journal of Postcolonial Studies* 16, no. 4 (2014): 483–500.

Jameson, Fredric. 'Political: National Allegory: Commentary'. In Fredric Jameson, *Allegory and Ideology*, 187–216. London: Verso, 2019.

Jameson, Fredric. 'Third-World Literature in the Era of Multinational Capitalism.' *Social Text* 15 (1986): 65–88.

Jameson, Fredric. *The Antinomies of Realism*. London: Verso, 2013.

Laachir, Karima, Sara Marzagora, and Francesca Orsini. 'Significant Geographies: In Lieu of World Literature.' *Journal of World Literature* 3, no. 3 (2018): 290–310.

Lazarus, Neil. *The Postcolonial Unconscious*. Cambridge: Cambridge University Press, 2011.

Löwy, Michael. 'L'Irréalisme Critique.' *Actuel Marx* 45 (2009): 52–65.

Orsini, Francesca and Laetitia Zecchini. 'The Locations of (World) Literature: Perspectives from Africa and South Asia.' *Journal of World Literature* 4 (2019): 1–12.

Rothwell, Phillip. *A Postmodern Nationalist: Truth, Orality, and Gender in the Work of Mia Couto*. Lewisburg: Bucknell University Press, 2004.

Salih, Tayeb. *Season of Migration to the North*. London: Heinemann, 1969.

Sousa Santos, Boaventura de. 'Between Prospero and Caliban: Colonialism, Postcolonialism, and Inter-Identity.' *Luso-Brazilian Review* 39, no. 2 (2002): 9–43.

Warwick Research Collective. *Combined and Uneven Development: Towards a New Theory of World-Literature*. Liverpool: Liverpool University Press, 2015.

Young, Robert J. C. 'Postcolonial Remains.' *New Literary History* 43 (2012): 19–42.

DAVID BROOKSHAW

2 From Nation to Imagination: Mia Couto and Language in a Comparative Perspective

The purpose of this article is to consider three writers from very different backgrounds and geographical locations, in light of their thoughts on nation, literature and its role in defining or evoking national identity, and their relationship with language. My focus will be, primarily, the polemical works of Mia Couto, Brian Castro and Jhumpa Lahiri, although there will be references to the fiction of these three writers. I start off from the premise that, despite their different life experiences, all three of these writers challenge established views of national and personal identity based on one accepted monolithic truth, and in which language and its function in expressing this identity have an important part to play.

In the case of Mia Couto, born and brought up in Mozambique to immigrant Portuguese parents, his writing has always questioned the accepted interpretations of what Mozambique was and is, either in the context of FRELIMO's early Marxist-Leninist doctrine, and even more so in that of present-day inscriptions of African authenticity, with its implied debarring of people of non-Mozambican African ancestry from truly belonging to the country. In his fiction, Couto has always carved out a space for the human dramas of characters representing Mozambique's minority communities (for example, the Indian in *Sleepwalking Land*, the Goan, Muslim, Chinese in *Voices Made Night*, and the old white colonial left behind in *Under the Frangipani*), or those Africans who were somehow co-opted into colonialism or co-existed with it (the game trackers who worked for the colonials, the former assimilated families in various novels and stories). But it is in his speeches and essays, subsequently collected and translated in *Pensativities: Essays & Provocations*, that he speaks more directly about what type of Africa African writers should write about, as well as the cultural realities and contradictions of modern Mozambique.[1] Before elaborating on this, we need to distinguish between Mia Couto and the other two writers we are going to consider. Unlike both Castro and Lahiri, Mia Couto is not a member of a diaspora, in the sense that he lives in and identifies with the country where he was born and brought up by parents, who were sufficiently liberal to identify themselves to a large extent with the country's fortunes after it gained independence from Portugal. The actual drama of physical uprooting, the act of migration with all its emotional effects, is something that he did not witness. Yet his preoccupations with the pluralities of identity and language place him alongside these other two writers, which invites us to reconsider what we mean by a diaspora, or re-define it as something more abstract, or even ignore the term.

Brian Castro, for his part, was born in Hong Kong in 1950 to complex Portuguese and Anglo-Chinese parentage, with a connection through his father's side of the family to Macau and the Shanghai Portuguese community of the 1930s. He has, however, been resident for most of his life in Australia, where he was sent in 1961. Like Couto, he has published novels which evoke his complicated relationship with his adopted country and his own ancestry, while in his essays, he takes issue with Australia's traditionally limited, monochrome vision of itself as a country based firmly in its Anglophone and Anglo-Celtic cultural heritage. At the same time, his adopted country has a complicated relationship with him as an Australian writer, for Castro has tended to be pigeonholed as Asian, and as such has often been invited to speak on Asian literature. Castro, in some sense, is caught between worlds, and writes interestingly on Australianness and on Asianness, this latter being a blanket concept which white Australians have bought into, much as Africanness is a European invention.

Jhumpa Lahiri belongs to another generation of cosmopolitan Indian, or 'Indo-politan', writers. Born in London in 1967, she moved to the United States at the age of two with her Bengali parents, who were originally from Calcutta. So, unlike Castro, who was sent ahead to Australia at the age of

1 Mia Couto, *Pensativities: Essays and Provocations* (Windsor Ontario, Biblioasis), 2015 (the English translation of a selection of essays and polemical pieces, previously published in *Pensatempos: Textos de Opinião* (2005), *E se Obama Fosse Africano? E Outras Intervenções* (2009), and *Pensageiro Frequente* (2010).

eleven to go to boarding school, Lahiri was brought up in an Indian immigrant family environment, but is effectively an American. Her novels and short stories reflect her autobiography and her dual inheritance, her fiction criss-crossing worlds between America and the Indian sub-continent. The success of her novel, *The Namesake*, which was turned into a film, put her at the forefront of a whole generation of writers who have emerged from the post-1965 current of immigration into the United States, and which includes writers of Latin American, Caribbean, South and East Asian, and African origins. But it is in her most recent work, *In Other Words*, that she writes most explicitly about the intricacies of language and identity, and the notion of one's identity as being not so much tied to a particular place, but to a set of life experiences.[2]

Africanness and Asianness

In his work as a biologist, Mia Couto, though a product of an urban environment, has travelled widely in rural Mozambique, and is acutely aware of the chasm that exists between the city and the country, the entangled patchwork of cultures that extend throughout the nation's territory, and at the same time, the hybridities produced by the clashes between urban modernity and traditional rural civilisation, and the paradoxes involved, of which there are numerous instances in his fiction – to cite just one example, the witchdoctor in *O Outro Pé da Sereia* (2006), who has a mobile phone, which he cannot use because he lives in such a remote area that he cannot pick up a signal. In various public forums, Couto has criticised those who seek to promulgate some sense of African authenticity, which nowadays takes the form of an unwritten conspiracy between European views of Africa, which differ little from those developed in colonial times, and the acceptance of these views by Africans themselves in their efforts to take pride in being African. Such notions of African authenticity have

2 Jhumpa Lahiri, *In Other Words* (London, Bloomsbury), 2016.

been incorporated into a Mozambican brand of nationalism that is exclusive rather than inclusive. At an address given in Cape Town in 2002, and published as 'What Africa does the African Writer Write about?' Couto stated: 'We need to escape from this trap, and that can only be done by those Africans prepared to accept, without fear, their membership in a culturally mixed world'.[3]

The focus for Brian Castro's criticism of the blanket term Asian is not so much Europe, or any former colonial power within the continent, but the surrogate European colonial power, Australia, which has inherited views of itself in relation to the outside world from Britain. The pigeonholing of Asia, a continent of multiple countries, cultures and languages, is as arbitrary as the monolithic view of Africa, made even more arbitrary by the inclusion of Russia as a European nation, even though its geographical extension as far as the Sea of Japan makes it as much, or even more so, an Asian country physically and a Eurasian country culturally. Castro's critique, in his essay 'Writing Asia' (1996), published in *Looking for Estrellita*, is both similar to and different from Couto's critique of Mozambique.[4] For while Mozambique began its independence as a revolutionary nation, in which all ethnic groups were considered equal, it has become more traditionally nationalistic. Castro's Australia began life as a surrogate Britain, a white settler nation: 'Australia has had a long history of confusing the racial with the geographic and linguistic … Given that nations emerge out of an ambivalence about themselves … Australia has had to define itself against others. But the tendency has been that instead of defining itself, and realising itself as a continuously changing society, it has nostalgically yearned for stasis, drawing on a large number of myths which, while uniting segments of its population, retard its overall ability to absorb newness and deal adequately with others'.[5] This isolationist view still persists among certain sectors of its ruling elite, despite the fact that it has received a large number of Asian immigrants since the 1970s.

3 Mia Couto, *Pensativities*, 25.

4 Brian Castro, *Looking for Estrellita* (St. Lucia, University of Queensland Press), 1999.

5 Ibid., 145.

Castro's recipe for Australian renewal is to foster the learning and translating of foreign languages as a means to encourage cultural cross-pollination, and to counter the noxious effects of monoglotism, aggravated by the country's physical isolation from other countries in the region, unlike, say, the United States with its huge Spanish-speaking population: 'Other cultures and languages reinforce and enrich us by powerfully affecting and destabilising our familial tongue. We gain by losing ourselves'.[6]

Language and language

In his essay 'The Private and the Public', Brian Castro seems to distinguish between official, public language, and the language of 'minorities', between 'major' literatures – that is, the literatures of the accepted canons exported elsewhere, and 'minor' literatures (by implication postcolonial or so-called 'ethnic' literatures), which 'flow … into social, national and linguistic dissociations and disconnections. It is because this expression unsettles one, startles one with the residues of bilingualism and trilingualism that the traditional mind wants to suppress it, to prevent the rhapsodic cry and avoid change'.[7]

For Castro, this desire for change, belongs, as it does for Couto and for Lahiri, though expressed in marginally different terms, to another language that lies below the surface of the official, subverting it, and suggesting new freedoms and forms of creativity. This inner world, as Castro calls it, is what enables us to resist the 'official story', and is the worst enemy of totalitarianism. By way of example, he cites the student protesters in Tien An Mien Square, who spoke to the world in English, not just because the world's media were there, but, as he says, 'because for many of them English had become part of that inner world of expression; English had provided the possibility of being Other, of being anti-official, dissentious and private'.[8]

6 Ibid., 153.
7 Ibid., 90–91.
8 Ibid., 94.

Lahiri tells us that her first language as a child was Bengali, the language of both her parents in their immigrant home in America. But the language of her education, and in due course her social life outside the confines of the home, was English. She grew up, therefore, in the crossfire between these two languages, pressured by her parents to speak in Bengali in the home, but inevitably reacting against this as English became her own dominant language, and significantly the language through which she entered the world of literature, initially through her reading and then through her writing. Her way of carving out a new space for herself, an 'independent path' unencumbered by the past was to immerse herself in a third language, and in so doing, reject what she refers to as her 'mother' and 'stepmother' tongues.[9] This led to her publication of *In altre parole* (2015), translated into English by Ann Goldstein, and published as a bi-lingual edition under the title of *In Other Words*, an account of her learning Italian, living in Italy, and her abandonment of English as a language of literary expression – a kind of variant on Ngugi Wa Thiongo's decolonisation of the mind. Lahiri concludes that she does not know whether she will ever write in English again.

At the same time, for Lahiri, like Castro's young Chinese protesters of 1989, another language represented not only a casting aside of old structures of authority, but also a path to change and, by implication, a new form of creative expression. The idea of standing still is what she considers an impediment to the exploration of one's imagination. For her, standing still is Castro's stasis: 'The moments of transition, in which something changes, constitute the backbone of all of us. Whether they are a salvation or a loss, they are moments we tend to remember. They give a structure to our existence. Almost all the rest is oblivion'.[10]

Despite her growing familiarity with and love of Italian, it is still sufficiently foreign to her for her to remain free of the imprisonment of identity. Through Italian, she can thus lose herself, like Castro: 'I continue, as a writer, to seek the truth, but I don't give the same weight to factual truth. In Italian I'm moving toward abstraction … Writing in Italian, I feel that my feet are no longer on the ground'.[11]

9 Jhumpa Lahiri, *In Other Words*, trans. Ann Goldstein (London: Bloomsbury, 2016).
10 Ibid., 171.
11 Ibid., 221

Mia Couto's image on the liberating potential of language could not be more similar to Lahiri's and Castro's. Like Castro, he lauds multilingualism among Africans, just as Castro had extolled the multilingualism of his cosmopolitan Luso-Asian father. Multilingualism is a manifestation of cultural pluralism, tolerance and broad mindedness. In his essay 'Languages we don't know we know', based on an address to a conference on literature and translation in Stockholm in 2008, Couto's case for plurality within the individual bears some resemblance to Castro's idea of the public and the private language, but unlike Castro, accepts both as having roles to play: 'Alongside a language that makes us part of the world, there should be another that makes us leave it. On the one hand, a language that creates roots and a sense of place; on the other, a language that is a wing upon which to travel'.[12] For Couto, there is the language we learn at school, the language of political authority (and in Mozambique, this of course is problematic given that it is a foreign import), but counterbalancing this, and subverting it is the creative, anti-authoritarian potential of Portuguese learned as a second language, transformed in the mouths and voices of Mozambicans, and thirdly, there is the language unencumbered by grammatical rules, the language that children learn and play with, the language of orality.

Language, storytelling and diaspora

Language is clearly a concern which binds these three writers together as a way of expressing their own plural identities. The hallmark of Couto's writing, especially his shorter fiction, is the creation of a new form of expression based on wordplay, neologisms and orality, inspired by the way Mozambicans might use Portuguese, with other languages occasionally appearing from underneath the blanket of an 'official' language. This is Couto's subversion of official discourse. Just as language is linked to orality, and orality to storytelling, stories assume a similar importance

12 Couto, *Pensativities*, 90–91.

in contesting the one overriding 'official' story. We are back to Castro's 'major' and 'minor' literatures, the individual or group stories capable of unwriting nations and creating new, alternative histories, based on, say, the diasporic experience. Yet, I began this paper by questioning whether diasporas should be redefined in light of Mia Couto's identification with the country of his birth and upbringing.

Unlike for both Castro and Lahiri, in Couto there is no personal backward glance at a world left behind, no nostalgia for or rejection of a world once lived in, even though certain characters in his fiction, such as the old Portuguese settler left behind in newly-independent Mozambique, or the Portuguese sergeant in his recent trilogy, *Sands of the Emperor*, are all haunted in their dreams by their past. Perhaps the best way of explaining the common experience of these three writers, is through their suggestion that we are all capable of containing diasporas within us. One of these is the temporal diaspora of childhood (Couto, for instance, often harks back to the wonders and stories of childhood growing up in Beira, and Castro recalls his own childhood in cosmopolitan Hong Kong as a time when his identity was unimportant, when no one asked him where he was from). But even more importantly, for these three writers, there is the diaspora of our imagination and creativity, evoked from the rootedness of our own physical world, the imagination that embraces change and an ongoing narrative, 'where we gain by losing ourselves' (Castro), where our 'feet are no longer on the ground' (Lahiri), 'that is a wing upon which to travel' (Mia Couto).

Works cited

Castro, Brian. *Looking for Estrellita*. St. Lucia: University of Queensland Press, 1999.
Couto, Mia. *Pensativities: Essays and Provocations*. Windsor Ontario: Biblioasis, 2015.
Lahiri, Jhumpa. *In Other Words*. London: Bloomsbury, 2016.

EWA A. ŁUKASZYK

3 Mia Couto and his African Context: Invention of an Origin

In an interview granted in 2015 and published as a part of *A Companion to Mia Couto*, the writer denies any commitment to the question of racial identity in African literature: 'I don't see colours in writing. I'm also blind to the issue of gender, which defends the idea that there is a masculine way of writing and a feminine way. I might understand the subject better if someone were able to explain to me what "black writing" is.'[1]

In strictly aesthetic terms, Mia Couto's position seems to lie beyond the boundaries of any possible debate. Nonetheless, the extra-aesthetic question of legitimacy of a white man speaking in the name of Africa appears as pertinent to the writer's local interlocutors, especially if we come back to the early postcolonial period and the beginnings of his literary path. Mia Couto and other Lusophone writers are confronted with the perception of a certain ambivalence in their personal stance. Being the son of a Portuguese couple who moved to the colony early in the 1950s, he had to face a specific sort of polemic at the moment of the publication of his first volume of short stories, *Vozes Anoitecidas*. As he admits, the racial argument was constantly present, explicitly or implicitly, in the mêlée:

> When *Vozes Anoitecidas* were published, some erroneous reactions took place. In Maputo, the capital of the country, some people asked questions like this one: 'If you can write Portuguese well, if you dominate standard Portuguese, why do you do this?' Other people went farther and said: 'You make fun of the persons who do not dominate standard Portuguese. You are taking ignorance for an exotic inspiration …' Others put the problem in racial terms, saying: 'O.K., you are white. How

1 Grant Hamilton and David Huddart, 'An Interview with Mia Couto', trans. David Brookshaw, in *A Companion to Mia Couto*, ed. Grant Hamilton and David Huddart (Woodbridge: James Currey, 2016), 15.

> do you know this? How can you speak of these things? What are your credentials to speak of these things that belong to the deepest cultural reality of the country, to the rural zones?'[2]

Certainly, Mia Couto is not the first or the only writer to deal with the paradox of African literature created by white authors. The question of literary and cultural 'credentials' to speak about 'these things' must be inscribed in a larger context of interrogations concerning the diversity of postcolonial society, both in Mozambique and from a transcolonial perspective of several countries arising from the disintegration of the former Portuguese empire. In Angola, the question of autochthonism, in reference to second-generation white settlers born in Africa and claiming solidarity with the very essence of the continent, has been creatively resolved in Pepetela's *Yaka*, a novel almost exactly contemporary with *Vozes Anoitecidas* (originally written in 1983 and published two years later). In this vision created by yet another white Lusophone writer claiming the right to speak as an African, the problem of the relationship between the settlers and the colonised land is symbolically resolved by an animist-like consubstantiation of the white child with the African earth: the new-born baby accidentally fallen from the hands of the midwife bites – or kisses – the dust. This consubstantiation is to be reaffirmed and completed at the moment of the hero's death. What is more, Alexandre Semedo, the white patriarch of an African clan, receives from his father a *yaka*, an equivalent of a tribal, animist idol that leads a life of its own, constantly observing and positively haunting his owner. Nonetheless, this sculptural representation of the coloniser is inscribed in the African pantheon of ancestors, constituting a symbolic acknowledgement of yet another African identity, a configuration of trans-generational continuity that also the white men establish.

Both Pepetela's and Couto's writing has often been debated in terms of 'magical realism'. The term, obviously adopted from quite a different geographical and cultural sphere (the Ibero-American one), is known to be a make-shift designation. David Brookshaw dismissed its pertinence in reference to Couto's writing claiming that it is merely 'a lazy, journalistic term'.[3] Instead of establishing a parallel with the supposedly

2 'Entretien avec Mia Couto', *Cahier* 3 (1996), 115.

3 David Brookshaw, 'Mia Couto in Context', in *A Companion to Mia Couto*, 18–19.

'magical' Ibero-American belief system, he suggests we should examine the larger horizon of Couto's literary inspirations, that go from Juan Rulfo to Graciliano Ramos, as well as the specifically Portuguese tradition of *crónicas*, short narrative pieces in close connection with daily life. Eventually, the term 'animist realism' might be proposed instead, since it connotes a precise, localised inscription in a well-defined system of beliefs, not a vague and supposedly universal 'magical' world view. Yet the question of legitimacy is still a central one. Both Pepetela and Mia Couto are persons with a specific cultural background lacking an intimate connection with such a system of animist beliefs and ritual practices. It is more pertinent to speak of a modern appropriation of animism marking the process of building a distance in relation to the Portuguese colonial legacy. As the coloniser's identity is rejected and deconstructed, the issue of the apparent absence of roots needs to be creatively addressed. The relative newcomers to the African universe try to replace those severed roots, to develop new ones by literary means.

The construction of autochthonism in Pepetela proceeds by a curious transformation of the patriarchal pattern of Portuguese colonisation. Alexandre Semedo is presented as a founder of a mixed clan. This new blood line connects the colonial past with an open, transformative destiny of African independence. His solidarity with the *yaka*, the shared voicelessness of the man in silent conversation with the idol, marks the end of a certain hegemony: the right to speak (and to give orders) that this particular patriarch renounces. Although immersed in history accelerating its pace throughout the convulsions of the dying empire, Semedo participates, as if only half-alive, in the non-historical mode of existence of an animist ancestral spirit. Finally, the mixed status of the idol is patent in the fact that it derives, at the same time, from the powerful tradition of African sculpture, its way of representing reality, and from the personage represented, who happens to be the white coloniser. Sculpting his image – that is rather an icon marked by a 'real presence' than a portrait in the Western sense of the term – the African artist acknowledged the coloniser's presence and perhaps, indirectly, his right to existence as a part of the African universe. Although the presence of the *yaka* is a haunting, disquieting one, the ancestors of Semedo gained a degree of recognition through the representation; the idol transferred from father to son offers an animist foundation to the new, racially mixed clan of Semedo's descendants.

Um rio chamado tempo, uma casa chamada terra, Couto's novel published in 2002,[4] still presents notable similarities with the narration of Pepetela. Once again, the white African writer deals with the problem of foundation and legitimacy, which is solved by creating a singular system of animist representation and affiliation. This time, one might say, it is all about a sort of animist literacy, the cultural competence giving the right to move freely among the ancestral spirits. Mariano (or Marianinho to distinguish him by a diminutive from the older generation) is a young man who returns to the village after a period spent at school, only to face a peculiar problem that requires from him rather the animist literacy I have mentioned than the modern competence acquired through formal education: his grandfather is believed to be neither dead nor alive. This is why the burial ceremony has been suspended; unexpectedly, Marianinho is asked to perform the rites, although in traditional terms he is still unfit for the task owing to his young age. The roof of Nyumba-Kaya, the house representing unity of northern and southern parts of the country, has been removed for the mourning, in a climate of generalised crisis and hardship. As the domestic ambiance is grim and heavy with unspoken truths, the presence of the boy epitomises a new hope. His innocence and purity contrast with unclean compromises made by the previous generation. This may be the reason why it is his role to serve as a medium receiving strange letters that, although written by his own hand, are believed to transmit the voice of the (un)dead grandfather. Such a transmission introduces a novel dimension of animist literacy. The act of writing connotes more than just personal creation, as would be the European understanding of the process. It opens a new channel between the living and the *xicuembos* (ancestral spirits worshipped by the family). As Marianinho can read in the first letter, 'each man is all the others. And the others aren't just those who are alive. They're also the ones who've crossed over, our dead. The living are voices, the dead

4 Mia Couto, *Um rio chamado tempo, uma casa chamada terra* (Lisbon: Caminho, 2002).

are echoes.'[5] Couto's legitimacy as an African writer is based precisely upon this claim of provoking an ancestral resonance, making the silent dead speak as an echo woken up by the voice of the living.

As I have suggested above, the racial question, apparently alien to the domain of aesthetics, penetrates nonetheless into the domain of literature. The doubts or objections presented to Mia Couto in the heat of the polemics accompanying the publication of *Vozes Anoitecidas* cannot be dismissed as 'erroneous', impertinent or illegitimate. Although Couto's writing gained ample space for reception in the circuits of World Literature, the globalised scholars and critics have no credentials to exclude from the debate the crude interrogations emanating from Couto's African interlocutors, for whom the paradox of the writer's race is indeed an important question to be explained or symbolically resolved. This is why a particular 'blood line' is established when the writer as a new patriarch engenders – in an extra-genetic sense – the figure of an African intellectual. Mia Couto hopes to become, just as Craveirinha or Honwana, the giver of an African literary legacy. What is more, becoming a *xicuembo* (ancestral tutor and protector) in a peculiar instance of writing, he strives to introduce a new strand into the literary genealogy. The hybrid figure of the animist intellectual would otherwise remain without *xicuembos*, unreconciled with the traditional outlook. The white writer tries to establish the missing connection, consolidating at the same time his own place and legitimacy in the African context.

The metaphor of extra-genetic transmission of blood, which the reader may regard as particularly far-fetched, is in fact deeply inscribed in both the writer's world view and his novelistic idiom. The double professional inscription of Mia Couto as a writer and a biologist is at least as significant as the racial ambiguity of being a white African author. He creates, so to speak, an animist scientific outlook, that one day might even serve as an inspiration for a new generation of African researchers. Namely, he affirms that 'biology is another type of language with which to gain intimacy with other beings. It's a way of reconquering our kinship with animals and

5 Mia Couto, *A River Called Time*, trans. David Brookshaw (London: Serpent's Tail, 2008), 40. For the core of the present analysis, I have worked with the original version of the novel.

plants.'[6] The sentence, although obviously taken out of its context, suggests the complexity of the notion of kinship in the universe of Mia Couto. It is not by chance that one of the secondary characters of *Um rio chamado tempo* bears the disquieting remembrance of the fact that, as a child, he had been saved by a blood transfusion from a white donor.

There also exists a link of extra-textual kinship between the author contributing to the modality of the Portuguese-speaking, novelistic genre (even if he explicitly rejects any complicity with the distinction between 'white' and 'black' writing), and the figure of the African intellectual blazing a trail for others to follow. With *Um rio chamado tempo*, Mia Couto paradoxically legitimises his origin by projecting his descendants. He places himself in the position of a forerunner, wishing to foster the emergence of a truly African intellectual, such as his character Marianinho, who incarnates the spirit of the African dead in a way that the white writer Mia Couto cannot. Establishing a new line in literary genealogy and initiating a chain of transmission, the 'white' voice presents itself as a mere makeshift solution, one of many interim instances and institutions of the postcolonial transition. In a way, such an attitude of giving up the hegemonic status may be compared to the speechlessness of Pepetela's patriarch, Alexandre Semedo, immersed in his silent dialogue with the idol. Yet paradoxically, through this operation of abdication and self-diminishing, Mia Couto gives a solidity to his voice. He announces the advent of a new writing figure that shall legitimise, *a posteriori*, his own status as a precursor and a sort of intellectual patriarch. Through extra-textual and extra-genetic paternity of Marianinho, his literary creation and the projected African voice of the future, Couto transcends the racial question imposed upon him by his Mozambican interlocutors. He wins the symbolic contest to which he has been challenged at the moment of the publication of *Vozes anoitecidas*.

The postulated link between the literary representation of the intellectual and his or her advent as a living figure brings me to muse on the cycle of lectures given by Edward Said in 1993.[7] Probably, it was not Said's intention to accentuate the link between the literary hero as a sort

6 'An Interview with Mia Couto', in *A Companion to Mia Couto*, 15.

7 Edward Said, *Representations of the Intellectual: The 1993 Reith Lectures* (London: Vintage 1994).

of prefiguration and intellectuals as real-life people. Looking back on his academic life,[8] he lamented that the requirement of speaking about literature, rather than real figures, was simply imposed upon him by academic institutions, unwilling, at a certain moment, to endorse his political engagements. Nonetheless, independently of the critic's original intention, the idea of the necessary link between the emergence of an intellectual and his literary prefiguration had been launched. The advent of the intellectual as a living participant in the cultural debate in Africa may in fact be conditioned by the previous definition of his or her status, prerogatives and mission inside the novelistic discourse, a discourse that, as suggested above, is not taken by its African receptors as something entirely fictitious and missing any articulation with 'real life' – at least not to the same degree as we are trained to believe in the West.

Marianinho may be identified as an emergent intellectual, who, according to Edward Said's definition, is an individualised figure endorsing and triggering cultural change through his mastery of language ('knowing how to use language well and knowing when to intervene in language'[9]), and even more specifically, through his masterful literacy. As the native African cultures are eminently oral traditions, writing may appear, even in postcolonial times, as a culturally alien gesture and a prerogative of the white man. Yet earlier postcolonial reflection on the ways of rebuilding and developing cultural identities has shown that the living voice, unsupported by writing, is doomed to be silenced either by the instances of modernisation or by the traditional, precolonial figures of dominance; such is the case, just to give an example, in Ben Jelloun's *Moha le fou, Moha le sage*. The question of literacy proves to be crucial.

The intellectual's vocation is a solitary mission in which one man, as Couto's undead grandfather says, 'is all the others'. Its essential aspect, accentuated by Said in his *Representations of the Intellectual*, is the mediation between a subjective consciousness and a community: 'the intellectual is an individual endowed with a faculty of representing, embodying, articulating

8 Edward Said, 'Between Worlds: Edward Said Makes Sense of His Life', *London Review of Books* 20 (1998), <http://www.lrb.co.uk/v20/n09/edward-said/between-worlds> (accessed August 9, 2016).

9 Edward Said, *Representations of the Intellectual*, 15.

a message, a view, an attitude, philosophy or opinion to, as well as for, a public', in order to 'represent all those people and issues that are routinely forgotten or swept under the rug.'[10] In Couto's novel, such people and issues are many – for example, in connection with the murder that has not been sufficiently investigated. The young intellectual faces a personal risk that is in proportion to the financial stakes implied in the fishy affairs. Yet the fear Marianinho experiences seems to be connected much more with the supernatural dimension of his intimacy with the dead he is to represent. What keeps him in awe is the power of the energy flow to be channelled through his own pen, as he becomes a medium for 'an ancient voice' representing justice, the community and the land.

The mission of the intellectual has to do with the country's politics and history marked by a progressive decadence of the revolutionary ideals. But the crisis presented in the novel encompasses not only social, economical and political life. It takes a cosmic turn as the earth 'closes itself', preventing men from digging graves for their dead. This is how both life and death become impossible. As a consequence, the mission of the African intellectual stretches beyond the boundaries established by the secularised vision of European modernity. He or she becomes a figure of universal salvation, redeeming the world, a cosmic whole encompassing both the living and the dead.

One of the Reith lectures delivered by Said in 1993 had a significant title: 'Holding nations and traditions at bay'.[11] As the essayist suggested, the most important task of the emergent intellectual is to oppose solidly established discourse, such as the one affirming that national unity was achieved in the battle against the colonisers. These discourses become exclusive and dominant, introducing a new form of symbolic violence that comes from inside, not from any external source of oppression. In a recollection of the early times of Samora Machel, Mia Couto admits that a crucial error of over-simplification was committed:

> In the first years [of independence], there was a certain minorisation of the indigenous languages; the entities that are in fact languages were called dialects and

10 Ibid., 9.
11 Ibid., 19.

> treated almost with shame. For example, they could not be used at schools. [...] The approach was a well-intentioned one – there was a necessity of creating a unified nation – but its price was to postpone the vital debate on the multiple identities that the Mozambicans possess and should assume [...] with pride.[12]

The source of this unifying violence is local and apparently legitimate, yet this fact changes but very little in its oppressive nature. As Said suggests, the intellectual's duty consists in 'asking questions, making distinctions, restoring to memory all those things that tend to be overlooked or walked past in the rush to collective judgment and action.'[13] A critical attitude towards the adopted course of action and the values chosen and promoted by the political structure must lead to constant corrections. Only in such a way, may the diversity present in the country be harmonised and merged into a coherent formula of community. The main problem diagnosed by Couto is the imperfect unification of diverse ethnic elements; this is why Mozambique is symbolised by a common house, called Nyumba-Kaya in order to render its composite nature: *nyumba* is the word for 'house' in the northern tongues, while *kaya* is the correspondent term in the south.

The main line of argument in this chapter traces the process of invention of an origin performed by a white, blue-eyed descendant of colonial settlers inscribing his voice both in the context of postcolonial literature and in the complex socio-political reality of an African country. This double process involves Mia Couto in a modification of the Portuguese language, which arguably he tries to rebuild in such a way that it renders an African way of experiencing and conceptualising reality. The result is a highly peculiar and recognisable style. Yet at the same time, this rebuilding can hardly be understood as an interaction between the colonial language and any African speech in particular. Couto, as a descendant of the Portuguese, has no native tongue of his own; he has no direct link to any of the native tribal identities. This is why the whole project of rendering an animistic outlook through the transformation of the novelistic discourse may appear suspended in the void.

12 'Mia Couto contador de um país', in Tânia Reis Alves, *A minha pátria é Moçambique* (Lisbon: Guerra & Paz, 2017), 51.

13 Edward Said, *Representations of the Intellectual*, 25.

Be that as it may, the linguistic experiment of Mia Couto is probably the most debated aspect of his writing. His idiosyncratic expression seems to be, at first glance, the effect of a contamination between standard Portuguese and 'the African speech' in some broad sense. The objectives of this literary experiment are nonetheless less clear than in the case of a young, urban and cosmopolitan writer from Angola, Kalaf Epalanga, who complains in the introduction to the volume of *crónicas* (chronicles) *O Angolano que comprou Lisboa (por metade do preço)*:

> I am that cultural orphan that hardly knows how to count till ten in the language of his parents, their parents and so on. Mosi, vali, tatu, kuãla, five, six, seven, eight, nine, ekui …[14]

It is not hard to believe that Couto and Epalanga share similar goals in their attempts at introducing African words into the dominant, postcolonial Lusophone standard. They try to disrupt the solidity and the hegemonic status of the dominant tongue. While Epalanga ironically adopts the identity of a 'cultural orphan', lamenting the loss of his ancestral tongue (Umbundu) only to celebrate the contamination of both languages and cultural systems, Mia Couto stays close to the utopia of Lusophone transcultural metalanguage. According to centuries-old mythology underpinning Portuguese maritime adventure, such a fusion of the words collected by sailors and missionaries, acquiring an almost mystical value, would possess greater expressive potentiality than any colonial language brought from Europe. Only such a pluriversal speech transforming mutual incomprehension into a synergistic, infinitely complex system of expression would permit dialogue about all the intricacies of the world, including the intricacies of Mozambican reality, in which plural cultures do not only cohabit or coexist statically, but also create ephemeral patterns of interference in the mirror of individual awareness.

The dream of transgressing the multilingual condition of humanity after the biblical catastrophe of the tower of Babel played an important role in the very beginnings of the Portuguese expansion. As a response

14 Kalaf Epalanga, *O Angolano que comprou Lisboa (por metade do preço)* (Lisbon: Caminho, 2014), 14.

to the intellectual trauma of contact with such a plurality of peoples in the world, the idea of the recuperation of the Adamic language, an older Mediterranean legacy, gained a certain popularity in Portuguese humanist circles. According to the 16th-century utopianists, the primordial tongue of humanity, lost – due to the divine wrath – on the construction site of the tower of Babel, might be recuperated. As the Portuguese humanist João de Barros assumed in his *Diálogo em Louvor da Nossa Linguagem*, 'the language of Adam is still in the world; some ten words in one nation, twenty in another.'[15] If the Adamic language survives among the peoples, the multiplication of contacts could lead to its reconstruction, and thus to the recuperation of the original innocence of mankind. In the 16th and 17th centuries, and also later on, Portuguese exploration was supposed to bring about a breakthrough in world history understood as the divine economy of salvation: with the completion of the apostolic work, humanity was supposed to enter a millennial stage of prosperity, anticipating the apocalyptic paroxysm and the Final Judgement. For the heterodox 17th-century Jesuit António Vieira, this eschatological vision took the shape of a universal state under Portuguese patronage, encompassing humanity.

A miraculous transformation of mankind, with its universal spiritual regeneration, was supposed to come about through, among other factors, the inclusion of the words of different tongues in Portuguese. In this way, post-Babelian language was to be transformed into a pre-Babelian Adamic tongue, consubstantial with a sort of extended Portuguese. This dream formed one of the elements of the mission that had no exact analogy with any other European colonial project, neither in the 'white man's burden' of Kipling nor the French conceptualisation of *mission civilisatrice*. The Portuguese did not see themselves as the harbingers of civilisation; rather, they created the persuasion that they were to become a sort of mystical force transforming the world, mediating in the divine project of salvation. They saw themselves as a yeast of universal transmutation in which different cultural manifestations were to fuse into a novel, supreme order. To a certain degree, this system of belief survived the end of the colonial

15 João de Barros, *Dialogo em louvor da nossa linguagem* (Coimbra: Imprensa da Universidade, 1917), 19.

empire and is to be found in contemporary discourses of the Lusophony, where the belief in the transformative power of language is still to be found.

Mia Couto's writing might be seen as an epiphenomenon of the vitality of those ancient visions. Not only does he share the aspiration of representing Africa in the dominant language, but he also strives to bring about a fusion of cultural voices that was not achieved before the end of the colonial era. The writer belonging to the dominant linguistic sphere (writing in the former colonial language), like the hero he creates, becomes a medium transmitting the voices coming from an afterworld – ancestral native speech, still lying largely beyond the frontiers of writing. As a medium, Mia Couto epitomises the native cultures of Mozambique, and lets them resound in the background of the hegemonic language. He creates a prose that possesses a translingual quality, since the objective is to transform the dominant speech in such a way that it might at least partially reflect the linguistic image of the minor cultures, which in the postcolonial period remain subaltern to the hegemony of languages with a global projection and a strong tradition of literacy.

The modifications introduced by Mia Couto into standard Portuguese are situated on various levels: grammar rules, phraseology, word formation, vocabulary. The peculiar stylistics of this writer became the object of analysis at an early stage of his career. On the one hand, the studies aimed at defining the linguistic nature of the transformations introduced by the author, and, on the other, at delineating the ideological potential of such a procedure. Already in the 1990s, Inocência Mata claimed that the linguistic creativity implies in this case 'a new ideology of expression' and a peculiar 'stylistic philosophy'.[16] The writer returns to the source of the conflict between the hegemonic language and the subaltern orality, putting it on the stage once again. At the same time, he appropriates the unique cognitive modalities present not only in the local African languages, but also in an even more intricate whole that Mata defined as a 'complex of ethnic and cultural Luso-Indo-Sino-Arabian segments.'[17] At the same time, the African

16 Inocência Mata, 'A alquimia da língua portuguesa nos portos de expansão em Moçambique, com Mia Couto', *Scripta. Revista do Programa de Pós-Graduação em Letras e do CESPUC* 1, no. 2 (1998), 264.

17 Inocência Mata, 'A alquimia da língua portuguesa', 264.

scholar analysed the synthetic senses transmitted in the translingual expressions used by Couto's heroes, such as the sentence 'Vens pousar quem, ndlati?' from the short story *O dia em que explodiu Mabatabata* included in the volume *Vozes Anoitecidas*.[18] The specific construction of this sentence, characterised not only by code switching but also by the modification of the syntactic properties of the Portuguese verb *pousar* (that becomes transitive), is supposed to signify, in the scholar's optics, the helplessness of a man exposed to the dangers of war.

Um rio chamado tempo is also characterised by a rich translingual tissue. The function of the expressions in African languages cannot be reduced to mere signs of exoticism creating an aura of 'Mozambican-ness' (distinct from the notion of 'moçambicanidade' that the nationalists strived to define and illustrate). Local notions often form a parallelism, appearing as doubles of the names given also in Portuguese. Nonetheless, referring to the same content in two languages does not create a redundancy, but multiplies the connotations and adds layers of sense. The crucial example is the designation of the house becoming the symbol of the postcolonial national unity, Nyumba-Kaya, which is, as it has already been said, a juxtaposition of the words from the native tongues used in the North and in the South of the country. Other elements with double designation are apparently not so important; their double denomination reinforces nonetheless the pluralistic resonance of the text and accentuates the potential of seeing and experiencing the world in multiple ways. The bird called *pássaro-martelo* in Portuguese appears as well as *mangondzwane*,[19] and the same kind of strong alcohol is called *derrubadeira* and *xidiba ndoda*.[20] Nevertheless, not everything has plural designation; the elements of the animist world have untranslatable names, such as the term *xicuembos* designating the ancestral spirits of the family. The procedure could be analysed in terms of the 'politics of untranslatability' proposed by Emily Apter.[21] There are things and affairs that can be named in several languages and treated as mutually

18 Mia Couto, *Vozes anoitecidas* (Lisbon: Caminho, 1986), 47.
19 Mia Couto, *Um rio chamado tempo*, 27.
20 Ibid., 42.
21 Emily Apter, *Against World Literature. On the Poetics of Untranslatability* (London and New York: Verso, 2013).

transparent, as well as spheres lacking such a linguistic transparency, where the terms appear as unique, without any equivalent. Nonetheless, these terms also pierce the divide between languages and become encrusted in Portuguese, a language that reinforces its status of a postcolonial matrix.

When Miseirinha says: 'Este lenço eu fui dada na cidade',[22] the modification of the usage of active and passive voice in Portuguese reflects the difference in the concept of subjectivity experienced in Europe and Africa. The African subject constantly appears as *patiens*, suffering the influence of material and immaterial, natural and supernatural factors. In another fragment of the novel, the old woman is afraid not of falling, but of the condition of being fallen – 'ficar tombada'.[23] This state of helplessness, already put in the limelight by Mata, is not connected to the evil caused by other people, as in the case of the bombardment, but derived directly from the natural limitations of the human condition that appears as *tombada* at the deepest, ontological level. And this is not a reference to the concept of the fall in Christianity. Irresistible inclination towards the earth and death as the ultimate destiny of humankind comes from the cognitive resources of African cultures. It implies a readiness to accept the insoluble interdependence of human beings, as well as other forces of the material and immaterial world.

The most poignant example of translingual speech in Mia Couto appears with the girl called Nyembeti, a sister of the undertaker, who speaks no other than the ancestral tongue of poverty combining all languages: 'Mali! Ni kumbela mali.'[24] It can be interpreted as a sort of pidgin older than the Portuguese presence on the eastern coast of Africa, combining elements imported by sailors from the Arabian Peninsula. It is a sample of universal speech older than European colonisation and its mystical dream of pre-Babelian restitution. Yet the pidgin, in spite of its universality, does not bring any echo of Paradise or remembrance of the original purity of humankind; to the contrary, it reflects the eternal character of poverty as the original condition of human beings. It is significant that the bearer of

22 Mia Couto, *Um rio chamado tempo*, 31. Literal translation: 'I was given this scarf in the city'.

23 Ibid., 136.

24 Ibid., 161.

this primordial beggar tongue is a woman, presented through a game of oxymoron: she is dumb, and nonetheless she speaks; she speaks in an incomprehensible way, and yet she is universally understood. At the same time, the figure of young and attractive Nyembeti forms a counterpart to the old woman Miseirinha; they both represent humanity in its passive voice, the eternal *patiens* of history, expressed in a peculiar grammar.

Couto's experiment should be seen as a part of a larger landscape of translingual and transcultural writing. What appears as particularly valid and promissory in African literature is the exploration of various layers of accumulated pidgins, the result of linguistic encounters and free mixing. The literature in former colonial languages coexists with a growing wave of writing in local languages. In the interview referred to at the beginning of this chapter, Mia Couto refused to acknowledge the difference between 'white' and 'black' writing. The latter, nonetheless, may be defined by the open perspective of new paths of creation in the native tongue, just as it has been exemplified by Ngũgĩ wa Thiong'o, who abandoned English in favour of his native Gikuyu. Such a perspective is not valid for the descendant of Portuguese settlers who, in his translingual experiments, remains limited by his lack of an intimate link to any native tongue in particular. He cannot competently go beyond his strategies of incrustation of terms or expressions, building up his own systems of projected untranslatability. Couto's literary relationships remain Lusophone, Iberian, rather than African. Certainly, the map of those links is global, fostering in return the global projection of the writer, his paradoxical translatability in the major, hegemonic tongues. One might even say that his weakness as a writer in Africa is inversely proportional to his strength as a global author. Couto offers a synthetic vision of Africa that exerts a great suggestive power in distant reading, but his broad strokes may be less captivating for a reader already familiar with or immersed in the African reality, for his diction fails to render with sufficient precision the cultural intricacies. Delving into the idiosyncrasies of native language might make his prose less comprehensible for the global audience, which is why he adopts a synthesising rather than a particularising strategy.

The exploration of connections between Mia Couto and Ibero-American writing, resulting in somehow abusive usage of the term 'magical realism' in relation to his work, became widely accepted in the scholarship. Yet it is important to remember that those connections were initially interpreted by Gilberto Matusse in his academic dissertation defended in 1993 as a way of circumventing the European tradition ('contornar a tradição europeia'[25]) and evading literary Eurocentrism. At the same time, they are indicators of the paradoxical 'global limitations' of Couto as a writer who is interested in exploring transcontinental connections and analogies rather than idiosyncratic details of the African outlook.

Against the background of his highly imaginative ways of treating the Portuguese language, which even justified the publication of a specific 'dictionary' of his peculiar tongue,[26] it is difficult to discern the shortcomings; it would be even more speculative to speak about the opportunities Mia Couto has missed, the elements he could have introduced into his experimental language, but failed to do so. Nonetheless, in order to contextualise the extent of work on language that Couto has actually performed, it would be interesting to mention some specific achievements of oral narration that have served Africans as a means of developing and enriching the expressive potentialities of Bantu languages. Could these means be introduced into the written literature? Whether they could or not, an awareness of these unexplored possibilities can be thought-provoking. An example of a Bantu peculiarity that might eventually migrate from dramatic oral narration to the experimental African novel are the so called ideophones, elements without a strict equivalent in any European tongue. In her classical work, Ruth Finnegan defined the ideophone as follows:

> This is a special word which conveys a kind of idea-in-sound and is commonly used in Bantu languages to add emotion or vividness to a description or recitation. Ideophones are sometimes onomatopoeic, but the acoustic impression often conveys aspects which, in English culture at least, are not normally associated with sound at all – such as manner, colour, taste, smell, silence, action, condition, texture, gait, posture, or intensity. To some extent they resemble adverbs in function, but in actual

25 Gilberto Matusse, 'A construção da imagem da Moçambicanidade em José Craveirinha, Mia Couto e Ungulani Ba Ka Khosa' (Master's diss., University of Lisbon, 1993), 62.

26 Fernanda Cavacas, *Mia Couto: Brincriação Vocabular* (Lisbon: Mar Além – Instituto Camões, 1999).

> use and grammatical form they seem more like interjections. They are specifically introduced to heighten the narrative or add an element of drama.[27]

The awareness of how particular the linguistic nature of 'Mozambicanness' is may actually help to situate Mia Couto's experimentation in its specific boundaries. In fact, his literary diction, in spite of its brio, remains faithful to the deep structure of the Portuguese language that he penetrates and modifies without truly transgressing its frontiers. Certainly, he must refrain from exhausting the patience and competences of his Lusophone readers. But as a result, his experiment may be reduced to a kind of xenoglossolalia, resounding with the echoes of the alien speech, but failing to come down to its essence. The absorption of the local elements reinforces the Portuguese language, but it never abdicates its status as a global matrix; the hegemonic speech grows even more powerful, becomes a gigantic stomach digesting the otherness, without necessarily fulfilling the promise of liberation of which Inocência Mata had once spoken. There is no doubt that Mia Couto succeeded in creating a private universe of language, which is an inalienable right of any writer. He did not manage, however, to transcend the difference in status that defines not only colonial, but also postcolonial relationships. The literature that has been created in this way remains on the level of an idiosyncratic xenoglossolalia understood as a writer's own speech, but it does not fulfil the utopia of a transcultural common tongue.

Couto's short stories and novels are necessarily read nowadays in the context of a larger landscape of transcultural writing created, according to Arianna Dagnino, by transpatriate writers who overcome and deconstruct the sense of belonging to their homelands.[28] Mia Couto remains alien to this requirement of transpatriation and the creative dissolution of the link between the writer and his or her homeland, no matter if it implies that Mozambique is his postcolonial political homeland or that the Portuguese language is an anti-political, immaterial homeland in the

27 Ruth Finnegan, *Oral Literature in Africa* (Cambridge: OpenBook Publishers, 2012), 66 (the book was originally published in 1977).

28 Arianna Dagnino, *Transcultural Writers in the Age of Global Mobility* (West Lafayette: Purdue University Press, 2015).

tradition of Pessoa/Bernardo Soares. No matter how far he seems to go on the path of deconstructing the Portuguese language, Couto remains a writer of the Lusophony. His experiments in exploring the synergy of Portuguese and the Bantu languages situate him quite close to the old utopia of the post-Babelian reconstruction.

The task of mediation between the global public and the idiosyncratic systems of thought and expression produced by native African cultures is undoubtedly an important task, and it is yet to be done. Global transmission of that legacy would require an internal act of translation, implicit in the very process of African writing. But most obviously, this creative translation may be done only by a writer much more competent in African cultures than Couto. As a writer wishing to claim and accentuate his relationship with Africa, he relies on the strategy of inventing, rather than exploring, his origin. Mia Couto paints himself as a forerunner, initiating a process that will hopefully go on in the literature to come. Among his personal achievements, as I see them, one might mention a paradox: on the one hand, the surreptitious deconstruction of the hegemonic narration of the Portuguese, adopting the words and world views of all languages in order to perform a metaphysical fusion which brings us back to the immaculate beginnings of mankind. On the other hand, Couto's invention of an origin puts in the limelight something opposite, the maculate, shameful, dysphoric beginnings of people, languages and communities.

Works cited

Alves, Tânia Reis. *A minha pátria é Moçambique*. Lisbon: Guerra & Paz, 2017.

Apter, Emily. *Against World Literature. On the Poetics of Untranslatability*. London and New York: Verso, 2013.

Barros, João de. *Dialogo em louvor da nossa linguagem*. Coimbra: Imprensa da Universidade, 1917.

Brookshaw, David. 'Mia Couto in Context.' In *A Companion to Mia Couto*, edited by Grant Hamilton and David Huddart, 17–24. Woodbridge: James Currey, 2016.

Cavacas, Fernanda. *Mia Couto: Brincriação Vocabular*. Lisbon: Mar Além – Instituto Camões, 1999.
Couto, Mia. *Vozes anoitecidas*. Lisbon: Caminho, 1986.
Couto, Mia. 'Entretien avec Mia Couto.' *Cahier*, 3 (1996): 114–118.
Couto, Mia. *Um rio chamado tempo, uma casa chamada terra*. Lisbon: Caminho, 2002.
Couto, Mia. *A River Called Time*, trans. David Brookshaw. London: Serpent's Tail, 2008.
Dagnino, Arianna. *Transcultural Writers in the Age of Global Mobility*. West Lafayette: Purdue University Press, 2015.
Epalanga, Kalaf. *O Angolano que comprou Lisboa (por metade do preço)*. Lisbon: Caminho, 2014.
Finnegan, Ruth. *Oral Literature in Africa*. Cambridge: OpenBook Publishers, 2012.
Hamilton, Grant, and Huddart, David. 'An Interview with Mia Couto', translated by David Brookshaw. In *A Companion to Mia Couto*, edited by Grant Hamilton and David Huddart, 14–16. Rochester, NY: James Currey, 2016.
Mata, Inocência. 'A Alquimia da Lingua Portuguesa nos Portos de Expansão em Moçambique, com Mia Couto.' *Scripta. Revista do Programa de Pós-Graduação em Letras e do CESPUC* 1, no. 2 (1998): 262–268.
Matusse, Gilberto. 'A Construção da Imagem da Moçambicanidade em José Craveirinha, Mia Couto e Ungulani Ba Ka Khosa.' Master's dissertation, University of Lisbon, 1993.
Said, Edward. *Representations of the Intellectual: The 1993 Reith Lectures*. London: Vintage, 1994.
Said, Edward. 'Between Worlds: Edward Said Makes Sense of His Life.' *London Review of Books* 20 (1998). <http://www.lrb.co.uk/v20/n09/edward-said/between-worlds>.

PETER J. MAURITS

4 Worlds of Mia Couto: The Aesthetic of the Global

In his study on literary worlds, Eric Hayot highlights the 'complexity and slipperiness' of the signifier 'world'. Marvelling at its 'byzantine etymological history', and with apparent astonishment, Hayot writes that 'world' in the Oxford English Dictionary 'run[s] to some forty pages', and that its denotations include 'human existence; a period of this', 'the earth or a region of it', and 'the universe or a part of it'.[1] Citing mere surprise over the first denotation, because the 'spacial implications' of 'world' may be more obvious than the temporal ones, Hayot appears puzzled over the potential of 'world' to refer to both 'any self-enclosing whole' and to 'the largest possible versions of that whole [...], totality'.[2] Hayot is not alone in his anxiety about 'world' and its relation to totality. In the context of literary studies in which he operates, 'world' has been one of the central terms of the last two decades, predominantly due to its connection to the arguably most significant paradigm shift in that discipline after postcolonial studies – world literature. In that World-Literature debate, (comparative) literary studies' response to the 1990s sociological debates on globalisation, questions of 'world' and 'totality' were central. Indeed, already in 1994, Lawall warned that '[p]romising the world is risky business,' because it may 'turn [...] out to be much smaller than the globe'.[3]

This anxiety about the totality of 'world', then, may be considered symptomatic of a historical moment and, in this essay, I shall argue that Mia Couto's novel *O outro pé da sereia* (2006) is best understood from that perspective. Specifically, I will first show that the world came to be

1 Eric Hayot, *On Literary Worlds* (New York: University of Oxford Press, 2012), 38–39.

2 Ibid.

3 Sarah Lawall, *Reading World Literature: Theory, History, Practice* (Austin: University of Texas Press, 2010), 1.

understood as a global totality due to the socio-economic developments sometimes referred to as globalisation. Those developments, as I will subsequently demonstrate, influenced lived experience and the production of culture, and shaped a *global aesthetic*. In the third section, I shall illustrate this aesthetic using *Babel* as case study (Iñárritu and Arriaga 2006), followed by my discussion of *Sereia*.

The concept of globalisation

The question of why it is necessary to discuss the concept of 'globalisation' in 2018 strikes me as legitimate. As Gupta writes, the word first appeared in the Webster Dictionary in 1961 and somewhat later, in 1974, in the OED. It gained coinage in the academy at the end of the 1970s and beginning of the 1980s, where it replaced the then more popular terms of 'international' or 'world' or 'universal'.[4] The term 'globalisation', then, is far from new. However, as Gupta explains, the meaning of 'globalisation' shifted significantly over time. Initially, it referred either to 'the desire to develop the study of sociology in the USA as a world-embracing enterprise' or to the desire of 'US business leaders and management gurus to extend US business interests, and exploitation of resources and labour, to a global domain.' As the term became used in international politics, it was disconnected from those initial meanings. Especially important in this context, Gupta writes, was the Brandt Commission report, published in 1980, which aimed to tackle the rich/poor divide in the world, and called for the '"globalisation of policies" to counter the "globalisation of dangers and challenges"'.[5] Contrary to the advice of the commission, the IMF and World Bank began implementing so-called *structural adjustment* programmes – a package of political-economic measures that prioritises international businesses and their profits over national populations and

4 Suman Gupta, *Globalization and Literature* (Cambridge: Polity Press, 2006), 6–7.
5 Ibid., 7.

their needs. As a result, 'globalisation' came to be understood as the political-economic oppression of the poorer parts of the capitalist system. This, in turn, changed after the fall of the Soviet Union, writes Gupta, after which the uses of 'globalisation' 'sp[u]n out of control' and 'proliferated exponentially, essentially with the effect of firmly decontextualising it and neutralising its ideologically partisan affirmativeness.'[6] How widely 'globalisation' now signifies is illustrated by Al-Rodhan, who identifies 114 definitions of 'globalisation' – a plurality he attempts to resolve by suggesting his own definition.[7]

Arguably, then, a discussion of how 'globalisation' is understood is more necessary now than ever before. Although the term is now predominantly disconnected from its object or social referent, or the discreet social reality that it denotes, that reality does exist. Fairclough makes a similar point, and maintains that despite the many connotations of 'globalisation', it ultimately refers to an actual 'set of changes which are actually happening in the world.'[8]

It is highly debated what this 'set of changes' consists of, and a consequence of the differentiation in the debate on 'globalisation' is that it is no longer possible to discuss all elaborations of the term in the limited space available in the essay form. It must therefore suffice to identify and unpack my particular understanding of the concept briefly. For better or worse, the perspective that I adopt is that of the world-system as developed by Wallerstein. He argues that 'the social reality within which we live and which determines what our options are has not been the multiple national states of which we are citizens but something larger, which we call a world-system'.[9] This system is 'and always has been a world-economy. It is and always has been a capitalist world-economy'.[10] For Wallerstein, the

6 Ibid., 6–8.

7 Nayef R. F. Al-Rodhan, et al., 'Definitions of Globalization: A Comprehensive Overview and a Proposed Definition', Geneva Centre for Security Policy (2006).

8 Norman Fairclough, *Language and Globalization* (London and New York: Routledge, 2006), 4.

9 Immanuel Wallerstein, *World-Systems Analysis* (Durham and New York: University of Duke Press, 2004), x.

10 Ibid., 23.

world-system is fragmented because it consists of multiple institutions such as the nation-state, firms, households, as well as of different cultures and flows of capital and labour. Moreover, the system is fragmented because there is a fundamental division within the system, which Wallerstein calls core, periphery, and semi-periphery. This tripartite division refers in the first place to different ways of production in different locations. In core areas, quasi-monopolies with a relatively high reliance on technology as opposed to labour are the dominant mode, creating the possibility of high profits. Peripheral production is labour intensive, competitive, and thus less profitable. Semi-peripheral production consists of a mixture of both. However, because these three ways of producing are each other's condition of possibility, and even though the world-system appears to be fragmented, it is ultimately unified – a *world*-system – through 'the division of labour constituted within it'.[11]

What does 'globalisation' mean from this perspective? Most importantly, the term refers to changes in the world-economy. Partly in response to the declining economic growth of the 1970s, governments in alliance with businesses attempted to reduce the cost of production by reducing wages, input costs, and taxation (in particular Welfare-State taxation), and by calling for the opening of borders to free trade – free flow of goods and capital ('but not labor', Wallerstein).[12] Wallerstein even suggests that globalisation may be understood exactly as the call to open up borders to capital and commodities within the world-system. In this process, the function of the Nation(-State) in the world-system was drastically reconfigured from prioritising the wellbeing of citizens, to prioritising the profits of corporations. From the perspective of world-systems theory, such measures are a recurring part of capitalism, a politico-economic system that continuously goes through the three phases of opening new markets, market saturation, and 'globalisation'. Globalisation, in that sense, is not a new phenomenon. Nevertheless, the current globalisation, the one that is central to this essay, has new aspects. First, it is now motivated by the *neoliberal* (free trade) *ideology* and (at least initially) by the (free trade) praxis of the *Washington*

11 Ibid., 23.
12 Ibid., 86.

consensus. That is to say, the globalisation central to my essay is a *neoliberal globalisation*. In some sense, it can even be said that neoliberalism is globalisation, which is illustrated by David Harvey's definition of neoliberalism as

> [a] theory of political economic practices that proposes that human well-being can best be advanced by liberating individual entrepreneurial freedoms and skills within an institutional framework characterised by strong private property rights, free markets, and free trade.[13]

Second, this globalisation is new to the extent that, for the first time in history, the world-system, and the free flow of goods and capital in it, overlaps with the entire globe. The world-system under 'globalisation', then, is truly a *world*-system.

The aesthetic of the global

The changes in the world-system affected lived experience globally, although in drastically different ways due to the division of labour fundamental to that system. Changes in lived experience, in turn, affected the way culture was produced, resulting in what some have called a *global aesthetic*. At my time of writing, what this aesthetic may look like and what its functions are have been discussed at some length (Jameson 1995; Adesokan 2011; Herlinghaus 2013; Werbner 2014; Herwitz 2017).[14] And

13 The resonance of Harvey's definition with what I described as globalisation will be evident, although it should be noted that neoliberalism as an ideology has arguably existed since the 1940s, and only became a truly dominant *praxis* in the world at large after the fall of the Soviet Union. David Harvey, *A Brief History of Neoliberalism* (New York: Oxford University Press, 2005), 2.

14 Akinwumi Adesokan, *Postcolonial Artists and Global Aesthetics* (Bloomington: Indiana University Press, 2011); Hermann Herlinghaus, *Narco-Epics:* A Global Aesthetics of Sobriety (New York: Bloomsbury, 2013); Daniel Herwitz, *Aesthetics, Arts, and Politics in a Global World* (New York: Bloomsbury, 2017); Fredric Jameson, *The Geopolitical Aesthetic: Cinema and Space in the World System* (Bloomington: Indiana University Press, 1995); Pnina Werbner, ed., *Political*

unlike the definition of globalisation, over the course of three decades, the understanding of what a global aesthetic is remained relatively stable.

Writing at the start of the globalisation debate in the 1990s, Erlmann argues that world music is exemplary of this 'new aesthetic form of the global imagination.'[15] Until then, the dominant idea was that world music constitutes a multicultural-like plurality or a form of resistance. Guilbault, for example, had argued that world music is about different forms existing alongside each other, and Goodwin and Gore argued that world music is a way of resisting American Imperialism.[16] Erlmann, however, argues this is not the case, nor is world music a new style invented by publishers to create new sections in their record stores. Rather, it is an entirely novel and 'emergent way of capturing the present historical moment', which he suggests is at his point of writing still 'in the making.'[17] Essential to that form, he says, is that it involves 'the total reconfiguration of space and cultural identity characterising societies around the globe', by means of the central category of 'synthesis' – different formal aspects join in one work. The function of this aesthetic of the global, he suggests, is to 'articulate the inchoate feeling expressed by the 1990 AT&T commercial: "we are all connected." '[18]

Erlmann's writings about music and especially his position on the global aesthetic and its function have been influential for the studies on literature and film. In particular, the notions that a global aesthetic has not yet completed its formation, and that it involves the trope of the 'connection of everyone/everything', are recurring in elaborations of the topic. The prominence of the trope of connectedness is unsurprising considering its overwhelming presence in cultural production on all levels, from marketing

Aesthetics of Global Protest: The Arab Spring and Beyond (Edinburgh: Edinburgh University Press, 2014).

15 Veit Erlmann, 'The Aesthetics of the Global Imagination: Reflections on World Music in the 1990s', *Public Culture*, no. 8 (1996): 467–487.

16 Jocelyn Guilbault, *Zouk: World Music in the West Indies* (Chicago and London: University of Chicago Press, 1993); Andrew Goodwin and Joe Gore, 'World Beat and the Cultural Imperialism Debate' *Socialist Review* 20, no. 3 (1990): 63–80.

17 Erlmann, 'The Aesthetics of the Global Imagination', 468.

18 Ibid., 468.

to the diegetic. Two brief examples: 'Everything is connected' became the main advertisement slogan of the adaptation of Mitchells' 2004 novel *Cloud Atlas* (2012). In the film *I heart Huckabees* (Russel 2004), detective Bernard Jaffe (Dustin Hoffman) is hired to investigate the meaning of the life of the protagonist. In order to do so, he explains to his client that there exists a relation between everything in existence. Demonstrating, he takes a blanket and argues that it represents everything, and that every being, object, and atom is on the blanket somewhere. Summarising, he concludes, 'we are all connected. [...] We. Are. Connected. And we need to learn to see the blanket truth, all the time.'[19]

This experience of connectedness is also integrated in literary and cinematic form itself, as John Limon illustrates in his essay 'Novel at the Center of the World.'[20] On the basis of Newman's *The Fountain at the Centre of the World* (2003), Limon suggests that there is a new aesthetic emerging, and that its function is to understand the world as world. Or, as Tutek reformulated aptly, for Limon, the global aesthetic emanated ultimately from the 'need to create a way of perceiving a historically consequential whole, an operative totality [...] at the global level.'[21] This aesthetic, Limon claims, has not fully formed and it is unclear what the 'future of the global novel might be.' Nevertheless, he suggests, a number of characteristic formal aspects can be identified. I will briefly address three.

Fountain, which Limon calls the 'possibly paradigmatic global novel', narrates the journeys of three main characters – Evan, Chano, and Daniel. Evan and Chano are brothers, and Daniel is Chano's son. However, they do not know each other, live in different parts of the world, and grow up in different class environments. Eventually, their paths cross at an anti-globalisation protest in Seattle. What is remarkable for Limon, bringing me to his first characteristic of the global aesthetic, is that there is no suspense in the novel, even though there is the possibility to create it. For

19 David Russel and Jeff Baena, *I Heart Huckabees* (2004), Los Angeles, CA, 20th Century Fox Home Entertainment.

20 John Liman, 'Novel at the Center of the World.' *Electronic Book Review* (2008) (accessed November 13, 2018).

21 Hrvoje Tutek, 'The Form of Resistance', in *Globalizing Literary Genres*, ed. Jernej Habjan and Fabienne Imlinger (London and New York: Routledge, 2015), 262.

example, Limon says of the familiar relations between the three men that 'it might have taken [Newman] longer to reveal [these] relationships. (...) in the third section, an anonymous 'boy' is introduced in Costa Rica. But by the seventh paragraph, we are told that the boy is named Daniel, the name of Chano's lost son.'[22]

Limon explains this as follows: The lived experience of the 'unity of the globe', he says, in resonance with my discussion of globalisation above, is either that of 'God', or of the 'free trade' of international corporations. And it is worth highlighting at this point that the examples of Erlmann, *Cloud Atlas*, and *Huckabees*, all imagine unity with the help of some company – be it AT&T, the *Cloud Atlas* marketing team, or a fictional detective agency. Limon continues to say that the 'intention of corporations' is 'to obscure the truth; [hence] an anti-corporate global novel must be as clear as possible at every point.' A second characteristic of the global novel, for Limon, is homelessness. None of the main characters in *Fountain* is grounded in a geographical location, and the novel even ends with Daniel embracing his homelessness as a position of emancipation. Limon, again, connects this to the nature of international corporations. 'International trade', he says, 'in cahoots with national institutions, is itself homeless'. This resonates with lived experience in the world-system and correlates to the way characters are shaped. The fountain in *Fountain* is, arguably, the one counterpoint, and creates a centre in a world-system that does not itself have a centre. In some way, then, I would argue that the fountain, which in the novel responds to the positive and negative occurrences in the fictional world by spewing more or less, cleaner or dirtier water, is the protagonist of *Fountain*. Finally, a third characteristic of the global aesthetic for Limon is that the characters in the global novels are not really characters. This ties in with my suggestion of the fountain as protagonist, although for Limon it means primarily that the characters relate not via interaction, but systemically: in *Fountain* it is a world-system (partly in the form of an anti-globalisation protest) that bring the characters together.

22 John Liman, 'Novel at the Center of the World.' *Electronic Book Review* (2008) (accessed 13 November 2018).

If Erlmann writes at the beginning, and Limon writes in the midst of the debate on culture and globalisation, Beecroft writes from the far end of that debate. Nevertheless, his claims are remarkably similar.[23] He, too, argues that it is difficult to speak of a global aesthetic, because it might imply that there is a literary circulation that 'truly knows no borders' – a type of circulation that does not exist at this point. Nevertheless, he says, there is a 'fantasy of a world without borders', and there is lived experience of the world as totality. Hence, there is also a global aesthetic, which functions to 'convey our interconnected and polycentric world.' Like Erlmann and Limon, he suggests that this occurs most importantly on the 'formal level', and he identifies one narrative device in particular: multi-strand narration or 'entrelacement'. This type of narration combines different narrative strands in one work of literature, film, and so on, and it is worth highlighting that both *Cloud Atlas* and *Fountain* are multi-strand narratives. Beecroft adds that this is not a new narrative technique, and is already found a century ago in discussions of the French novel. However, in contemporary works that use multi-strand narration the different strands do not simply coexist but are interconnected. In his own words, 'what is new', Beecroft argues,

> is the use of this device as a way to project onto the level of form the paranoiac interconnectedness of life in a globalised era and the expansion of the scale on which these narratives are interwoven to the level of the planet itself.[24]

In other words, the different narrative strands are connected on the level of the story, establishing, to use Tutek's term, an operative totality within the work. To sum up, it has been argued over a period of at least three decades that there is an emerging aesthetic of the global, which has been considered a response to, an expression of the lived experience in, or an attempt to create a representational paradigm of the changes in, the politico-economic system that now involves the entire globe and thus constitutes the world as totality. To do so, several prominent formal elements have been identified, including synthesis of different styles, homelessness of characters who are not really characters, the absence of suspense,

23 Alexander Beecroft, *An Ecology of World Literature* (London: Verso, 2015), 39.
24 Ibid., 302.

and the use of multi-strand narration. In what follows, I will discuss *Babel* and *Sereia* at more length in the context of these formal devices.

Babel

The 'globality' of *Babel* is manifest in its production and form. Authored by the two Mexican producers, it involved French (Central Films), American (MRC/Paramount/Anonymous Content), and Mexican (Zeta Films) production companies, a cast of Mexican (Adriana Barazza, Gael García Bernal), American (Cate Blanchet, Brad Pitt), Moroccan (Driss Roukhe), and Japanese (Rinko Kikuchi, Koji Yakusho) actors, and it was shot on location in Japan, Morocco, the US and Canada. It was distributed by the US-American Paramount Vantage and the French Mars distribution. On the level of production, then, at least in some sense, *Babel* is homeless. Formally, the dialogues take place in Berber, Japanese sign language, French, Arabic, Spanish, and English. *Babel* is structured using the narrative device of multi-strand narration, with strands set in Morocco, Mexico, USA, and Japan, and it is therefore not surprising that Beecroft cites it as one of his main examples. These different narrative strands are interconnected in the plot, which can be summarised as follows: a Japanese man named Wataya gifts a Winchester rifle to a Moroccan man named Ibrahim, who sells it to his Abdullah, who gives it to his sons to chase jackals from the goats they herd. The boys accidentally shoot the American tourist Susan Jones with the rifle and wound her nearly fatally. The Joneses then have to stay longer than planned in Morocco (in a hospital), forcing their nanny in San Diego, the Mexican Amelia, to babysit longer, which threatens to make her miss the wedding of her son. She is persuaded to bring the Jones' kids to the wedding in Mexico, but loses them on the way back after being chased by the border police. Eventually, she is found by the border police and expelled from the United States where she had stayed illegally from the perspective of US law.

Writing about *Babel*, Kerr[25] highlights the importance of the circulation of objects to the film. Based on what I called the homelessness of *Babel*'s production process (which he discusses in great depth), he argues that the film 'was constructed by globalised, casualised labour, and assembled by international agencies and companies which circulate capital.' And he goes on to suggest that the way in which that production was organised is 'in much the same way as the circulating object, the Winchester, changes hands in the film.' *Babel*, in other words, is a narrative of circulation, a refraction of the functioning of the international corporations that also produced the film. Following Bordwell, Kerr therefore proposes to see *Babel* as a 'network narrative'[26] which is about 'crossing barriers', and in which the 'circulating object' is central.[27]

The circulation of the Winchester is indeed essential to *Babel*, and I would even suggest that in some ways, because it connects all characters (at least partially, as I will elaborate below), it is the protagonist of *Babel* in the same way that the fountain is the protagonist of *Fountain*. However, while the focus on the circulating object is informative, it ignores the *system* of circulation – that which engenders the circulation of the object, and which is the organiser, the condition, of totality in the work. One of the reasons I believe this is the case is not so much because of the focus itself, but the use of the term object. If we were instead to speak of the circulation of a (specifically US-American) commodity, it would highlight the existence of a world-system, the system in which commodities exist. And of course, it is in the globalisation, free-trade phase of the world-system that commodities (and not in the last place arms) can circulate relatively unobstructed. I would argue, too, that speaking of the circulation of commodities highlights those elements that do not circulate well in globalisation, namely labour. In other words, it draws our attention to the (lack of) mobility of the characters, which is as essential for the interconnection of

25 Paul Kerr, '*Babel's* Network Narrative: Packaging a Globalized Art Cinema,' *Transnational Cinemas* 1, no. 1 (2010): 39–40.

26 The term *network* was one among many used to explain the connectivity in the era of globalisation, and was popularized in that context by Manuel Castells in *The Rise of the Network Society* (Oxford: Blackwell Publishing, 1996).

27 David Bordwell, *Poetics of Cinema* (London and New York: Routledge, 2008).

the narrative strands and the plot in *Babel* as the Winchester is. Indeed, characters move the object of the rifle from one place to another.

Mobility (and specifically international mobility) in *Babel* is divided roughly in three categories. The Japanese character Yasujiro Wataya, who is an executive and the former owner of the Winchester, is situated in the first. Wataya's journey is located out of the narrative time, but the viewers know that he travelled to Morocco for a hunting trip, of which a photograph remains as proof. He is, in other words, a tourist, and is able to travel as he pleases. For a brief moment, it appears that his mobility is burdened by his complicity in the attack on Susan Jones. But when the police question Wataya, and it turns out that the gun was not the subject of a black market deal but a gift from him to Hassan Ibrahim instead, Wataya is exonerated of all guilt. Similarly, the US-American couple can travel as they please. They, like Wataya, travel to Morocco for their holiday and are thus also tourists. Even if their mobility is temporarily impeded – after Susan has been shot, she is unable to travel on by bus, and has to be treated by a local physician – this is counterbalanced by her subsequent transport in a US-American army helicopter. The border crossing potential of Amelia's character is more ambiguous. A migrant labourer, she makes possible the mobility of the Jones, whose children she babysits while the couple is in Morocco. Amelia, thus, does have mobility, but in a more precarious form, in particular because it is based in administrative illegality. After she loses the children, and has been released by the border police, she is not allowed to stay in the US any longer. In some way, then, the story line of Amelia is not so much that of her mobility, but rather of its destruction, as she is forced to leave the country that she has called home, and the children that she has called her own (not an unproblematic trope, as it echoes the 'mammy' trope), due to an incident that is ultimately not in her hands. Finally, the Moroccan characters do not have mobility, as is most clearly shown by the main household on which the film focuses. Initially, Abdullah's family has no desire to leave their area of residence, which is where they both work and live. However, after Susan Jones has been shot and it has become clear that the police know who the shooter is, this lack of mobility becomes evident. Abdullah and his sons try to flee, but they are intercepted by the police on the same mountain that the shooting took place on. One of the boys is even shot, fatally as it seems, and Abdullah and his second son are captured by the police.

Babel, then, is as much a film about the 'crossing borders' of commodities as it is about the unequal distribution of human mobility. More specifically, it appears that mobility in Babel is distributed unequally across a tri-point spectrum, which in some ways may be understood along the lines of Wallerstein's world-system – there is in *Babel* a core (the Joneses/Wataya), semi-periphery (Amelia), and periphery (Abdullah). It is worth highlighting that those whose movement is obstructed are all workers, and I would therefore suggest that we might speak of the restricted movement of labour in the context of the film. Further, I suggest that this juxtaposition of the mobility spectrum and the unobstructed mobility of the commodity are the key conditions for *Babel*'s plot to unfold.

Babel thus relies on the formal devices that have been identified in the context of the global aesthetic – homelessness, entrelacement, characters who are not quite characters. In addition, the organising structure of the work – the juxtaposition between the free movement of commodities and the unequal distribution of mobility among humans (and labour) – can be recognised as the organising structure of globalisation, in which borders are opened to goods and capital, but not to labour. Nevertheless, although these structures are present in the film, they are not presented as the operative totality, the structural logic of connectedness, in *Babel*. Rather, connection in *Babel* pivots on the children accidentally hitting Susan Jones in the bus, a combination of foolishness and chance, or foolish chance. In *Babel*, then, the operative totality is mystified as being foolish chance.

O outro pé da sereia

Sereia's connection to the global aesthetic is immediately obvious. Like *Babel*, *Fountain*, *Cloud Atlas* and so on, *Sereia* uses what Beecroft calls entrelacement, and establishes a connection between the different narrative strands. In brief, the story consists of three journeys (not unlike in *Fountain*). One journey takes place in 2002 and its protagonist is Mwadia. Living with her husband in a place called Antigamente, she returns to her hometown of Vila Longe to find a resting place for a Maria statue that she found close to her home. A second journey, also set in 2002, revolves around the Brazilian-Afro-American couple Benjamin and Rosie Southman, who travel from New York to Vila Longe in the hope to experience their imagined and exoticised version of Africa. Finally, the third journey takes place between 1560 and 1561, and involves a ship with African slaves travelling from India to Mozambique. On board is the Maria statue (the mermaid who lends her name to the title of the novel) that Mwadia will later find close to her home, and some of the passengers attempt to find a home for the statue. The 2002 journeys are joined in one narrative strand, and Benjamin and Rosie arrive in Vila Longe shortly after Mwadia does. The 16th and 21st century journeys are divided over two narrative strands, and are intertwined by means of the statue. An alternative summary of *Sereia*, then, could be 'the quest to find a home for the Maria statue, which passes through India and Antigamente, and ends in Vila Longe'. In the first instance, if we choose to limit ourselves to Limon's two categories for now, it would appear that everything in *Sereia* is connected through God.[28] The construction of *Sereia*'s world as totality, and the connections to the global aesthetic, however, is incorporated in the structure of *Sereia* in more subtle ways, as I will proceed to show.

Sereia is generally understood relative to the concept of globalisation. Madureira maintains that the novel is in 'accordance with the global economic logic [of neoliberal capitalism]'; Brugioni argues that the novel reflects on a 'globalised world'; for Monteiro and Nenevé the novel shows that 'cultural globalisation is also a form of colonisation'; and Lopes argues it is a narrative about global inequality.[29] This understanding is unsurprising

28 I should note that the significance of the statue modifies throughout the work. Starting as a Christian symbol, it eventually becomes an indigenous deity. Arguably, it would therefore be more accurate to speak of religion or culture rather than of God.

29 Elena Brugioni, 'O Outro Pé Da Sereia: História[s] Na Pós-Colonialidade.' *Luso-Brazilian Review* 49, no. 1 (2012): 46–62; Madureira, Luis. 'Nation, Identity and Loss of Footing: Mia Couto's *O Outro Pé da Sereia* and the Question of Lusophone Postcolonialism,' *Novel: A Forum on Fiction* 41, nos. 2–3 (June 2008): 200–28;

because the novel explicitly addresses the phenomenon of globalisation, as I argue in a forthcoming publication, in the different ways it has been theorised ('economic' globalisation, Coca-Colasation, the global village, creolisation, cosmopolitanism, and pan-Africanism). One scene in particular is cited in this context. After the Brazilian-American couple arrives in Vila Longe, Mozambique, the husband, Benjamin, 'balbuciou [...] com a voz prisioneira da emoção, "*Oh, Africa! My forgotten land!*"' [stammered, with a voice imprisoned by emotion].[30] Benjamin's exclamation is ambiguous, as it appears to reiterate the colonial representation of Africa as a 'dark continent', while its pathos seems to indicate that he instead wants to draw on the homeland paradigms of Cesaire's 'Cahier d'un Retour au Pays Natal' (1939) or Rushdie's *Imaginary Homelands* (1991). One character, Casuarino, has no trouble identifying this ambiguity for what it is. Beforehand, Casuarino planned to use the visit to earn some money for him and the village, to which the villagers do not agree. Nevertheless, seeing Benjamin's response, Casuarino positions himself in the middle of the square theatrically, climbs on his personal soapbox – 'uma grade de coca-cola' [a case of Coca Cola] – and in a similar vocabulary, 'em tom solene e eufórico, proclamou: – *Isto é a globalização, my friends! A globalização mundial! Vila Longe é a capital da aldeia global!*'. [in a solemn and euphoric tone, proclaimed: *This is the globalisation, my friends. The worldwide globalisation! Vila Longe is the capital of the global village!*].

The scene, in my view, is among the most accurate characterisations of the globalisation debate. It presents globalisation as shifting concept as it slips from a noun, to an adjectivised noun, to an adjective. As a logical consequence, the term's referent is unclear, and while 'globalização' should be clarified by the demonstrative pronoun 'isto', it cannot be said with certainty to what that demonstrative links. More importantly, the scene sets the tone for what globalisation means in the novel, in resonance with the elaboration of the global aesthetic above. As in *Fountain*, and in seeming opposition to the homelessness that characterises contemporary

Lucineide Rodrigues Monteiro and Miguel Nenevé, 'O outro pé da sereia, de Mia Couto: a desconstrução da visão eurocêntrica sobre Moçambique,' *Polifonia* 19, no. 26 (2012): 52–62.

30 Mia Couto, *O outro pé da sereia* (Lisbon: Caminho 2006), 168.

capitalism, Casuarino suggests that globalisation has a centre, i.e. Vila Longe. However, in *Fountain*, the centre is a narrative device on the level of the zero focaliser, which lies outside of the diegetic agency – the omniscient narrator, who is outside of the diegetic world, and steers the reader back to the behaviour of the fountain over and again. The establishment of Vila Longe as the centre of globalisation, on the other hand, is a (succinct) marketing campaign by Casuarino, who, I suggest, we may best see as the town's advertiser. Globalisation in *Sereia*, in other words, revolves around international exchange, or is even a tool to propagate exchange, connecting to Limon's second notion of the lived experience of globalisation as free trade. It is symbolic, in this context, that Casuarino makes his declarations about globalisation from the platform of a crate of the Coca Cola Company – the multinational par excellence.

This trope, *exchange as totality*, runs throughout the novel. Before Benjamin and Rosie's arrival in Vila Longe, the reader learns that the couple, and Benjamin in particular, wants to experience an exoticised, authentic Africa, 'a sua África' [his Africa].[31] Casuarino, possibly experienced in these matters, anticipates the wishes of the two tourists, and is willing to play along because it will result in 'algum pagamento' to the villagers.[32] It is 'simples' [simple], Casuarino argues, pushing the exchange trope *ad comicum* through the repetition of the verb 'pay': 'os tipos vão pagar. Vão pagar para ficar numa casa, pagam pela comida, pagam pela estadia, pela informação … todos vamos ganhar o taco respectivo. […] Eles gostam de pagar'[33] [those types will pay. They will pay for staying in a house, for food, for their stay, for information … all will gain their respective part. […] They love paying]. And when Benjamin tells Matambira that they can only pay to local organisations, Casuarino urges him to tell the American that 'nós é que somos uma comunidade autêntica e autenticada, nem você encontra aqui mais nenhuma' [we are an authentic and authenticated community, nor will you encounter another one here] (176).

31 Ibid., 161.
32 Ibid., 175.
33 Ibid., 152.

In order to create this authentic Africa, several forms of entertainment are organised for the Southmans, such as a séance and a naming ceremony. In the first, the villagers themselves are uncertain if Mwadia is really a medium possessed by spirits (the reader later finds out that Mwadia bases the sessions on historical documents that she has found). For the couple, however, the ritual connects flawlessly to their exoticised image of what Africa is, and they have no doubt that it is real. As Casuarino 'previra, os americanos ficaram fascinados com a sessão de transe. – Eis África autêntica, repetiam, deleitados'[34] [foresaw, the Americans were fascinated by the trance session. – This is authentic Africa, they repeated, delighted]. The customers, in other words, are satisfied. With the naming ceremony it becomes clear that Benjamin's desire is not simply to consume 'his' authentic Africa, but to become part of it. Towards the end of the novel, he tells the villagers that he wants to take part in a ritual to acquire a new, African identity. The villagers do not agree, to which Benjamin immediately responds, 'eu pago' [I'll pay].[35] The villagers indicate that this time it is not about money: 'Não falo de dinheiro. Falo de custos' [I am not talking about money. I am talking costs].[36] Nevertheless, Benjamin gets his way, and shortly after, villager Singério tells him that the ceremony will be one day later. Benjamin is still not satisfied and wants to know his new name directly, which is followed by a back and forth between Benjamin and Singério:

> [Singério] 'Não posso.' [Benjamin] 'Eu pago.' 'Nada. Não posso.' 'Eu pago muito.' Benjamin foi aos bolsos e retirou uma nota. O outro sacudiu a cabeça, em negação. Do colete saiu uma mão cheia de dinheiro. [...] 'Dere Makanderi.' 'Como?' [...] 'Primeiro, o dinheiro.' Southman entregou o molho amarfanhado das notas ao mesmo tempo que insistia: '*o nome, depressa, o nome!*' 'Dere Makanderi.'[37]
>
> [Singério] 'I can't.' [Benjamin] 'I'll pay.' 'No. It's not possible.' 'I'll pay a lot.' Benjamin reached for his pockets and grabbed a bill. The other shook his head, in negation. From his vest he grabbed a handful of money. [...] 'Dere Makanderi.' 'What?' [...] 'The money first.' Southman handed the wet and rumpled money and at the same time insisted: '*the name, quick, the name!*' 'Dere Makanderi.'

34 Ibid., 276.
35 Ibid., 318.
36 Ibid., 318.
37 Ibid., 333.

If exchange is part of what connects the characters in *Sereia*, I should emphasise that this form of exchange is not free trade, as Limon suggests, per se. Rather, the exchange that connects the couple (and especially Benjamin) and the villagers is that of the petty commodity production of the informal economy. For Wallerstein, it is 'obvious' that 'this sort of production continues to be very widespread in the poorer zones of the world-economy.'[38] In the richer parts, wages are sufficient for subsistence, while in the periphery wages are lower and may need to be substituted by other forms of income. The informal economy, thus, is a function of the international division of labour of the world-system, and it is that division of labour, rather than in the first place free trade as Limon suggests for *Fountain*, which in part establishes the operative totality in *Sereia*.[39]

The naming ceremony of Benjamin leads me to a final device of the global aesthetic that plays an important role in *Sereia* – homelessness. Benjamin and Rosie are 'Afro-Americano' (10), he considers himself an African descendant, his wife Rosie is from Brazil, and while their last name is Southman, they live in the north, in New York. Benjamin is not satisfied with his fragmented identity, feels African, and wants to become African officially through the naming ceremony. However, although it appears that the north-living, Afro-American, African feeling Benjamin Southman wants to shed the homelessness that is pulling his identity apart, receiving his African name has the opposite effect. After Singério tells Benjamin his new name is Dere Makanderi, Benjamin thinks, '"Já não sou afro-americano" [...]. Agora que tinha um nome novo, pouco lhe interessava pertencer a uma identidade maior. [...] Ter pátria, ter raça, nacionalidade: que importância tinha?' ['"I'm not an African-American anymore" [...]. Now he had a new

38 Wallerstein, *World-Systems Analysis*, 33.

39 The connection between the three different journeys is established in many ways throughout the novel. The examples are too numerous to discuss, but because they are relevant to my argument, I will highlight one. After Benjamin acquires his new name, he walks on to a pier, and the narrator interrupts the story to point out that 'O americano não sabia, mas tinha sido naquele mesmo cais que, há mais de um século, o capitão-mor do Zumbo – o português José Pedro – acorrentara dois jovens a uma canoa e os lançara na correnteza' (Couto, *O outro pé da sereia*, 335). The relevance of this scene is precisely that there is no relevance; the only function this part seems to have is pointing out that everything is connected.

name, he was no longer interested in belonging to a larger identity. [...] To have a fatherland, to have race, nationality: why was this important?'.[40] Benjamin, then, arguably becomes *more* homeless by getting a new identity.

Another homeless character that is not quite a character is the Maria statue; the sereia which gives the novel its title. It was mentioned above that *Sereia* may be summarised as the quest to find a home for the Maria statue (the sereia in the story), signalling the centrality of the homelessness trope in the novel. More precisely, it would make *Sereia* a novel about ending homelessness, which in some way would make the statue the protagonist of *Sereia*, in the same way that the fountain is the protagonist of *Fountain*, and the Winchester that of *Babel*. I would therefore suggest considering this *object-as-protagonist* as an additional characteristic of the global aesthetic. Mwadia indeed finds the statue a home at the end of the novel, at a 'largo embondeiro' [large baobab] (379). Of course, as soon as the statue has found a home, Mwadia herself becomes homeless. Returning from Vila Longer to Antigamente after laying the statue to rest, she decides to leave that place behind, apparently for good. The novel ends with substantial Coutoian symbolism. Mwadia leaves her former home for an unknown destination: she 'tomou o caminho do rio' [took the path of the river]'.

Conclusion

My conclusion is simple: I suggest that Mia Couto's *O outro pé da sereia* is best understood in the context of the global aesthetic. This formal paradigm started emerging during the 1990s, developed throughout the first two decades of the new millennium, and expresses in a refracted way the lived experience of the now global (unequal) totality of the world-system. In *Sereia*, this is illustrated by the use of narrative devices associated with this global aesthetic, including multi-strand narration, interconnection of those multiple narrative strands, the use of God and (international)

40 Couto, *O outro pé da sereia*, 335–336.

exchange to establish an operative totality, the not-quite-a-character characters, and the centrality of homelessness. I suggest the *object-as-protagonist* as an additional characteristic of the global aesthetic.

It is necessary to add, I believe, that this does not mean that *Sereia* and other works using the global aesthetic blend into a homogeneous mass. It does not mean either that *Sereia* does not have, or does not participate in, specifically 'Mozambican' literary aspects, conventions, or traditions, even if I have not highlighted them. At a minimum, works employing the global aesthetic may be characteristic of their location within the world-system, which is differentiated by an international division of labour. The examples above demonstrate this, as they all employ the same formal devices but offer different perspectives.

I believe this to be a necessary addition because the anxiety about the global aesthetic and the possible ultimate dystopian horizon of homogenisation of all cultural production is inherent to discussions about that aesthetic. This is both understandable and justified, because as Jameson showed, a certain homogenisation has been established in global cultural production.[41] This anxiety may also explain the continuous emphasis on the global aesthetic's status as emerging. That openness to the future, it seems to me, functions as a warning. As an aside, it may therefore be useful to speak of a *pre-global aesthetic* instead, thus marking the possible dystopian horizon within the category itself.

Finally, there may be a consequence to this conclusion. As discussed, the dominance of the neoliberal ideology and practice over the last thirty years has drastically changed the organisation of the world-system and the (functions of the) nations within it. Correlative to these changes, literary worlds, including those of Mia Couto, also modified, and I would wager that this claim could be expanded to Mozambican literature at large. In other words, a shift has taken place from 'nation' to 'world', or better, to world-system, or perhaps even, from 'world as nation' to 'world as world-system'. This shift has not always affected the study of Mozambican literature as drastically as could be expected, and the category of the 'nation'

41 Fredric Jameson, 'Notes on Globalization as a Philosophical Issue,' in *The Cultures of Globalization*, ed. Fredric Jameson and Masao Miyoshi (Durham and New York: University of Duke Press, 1998).

uninflected by that shift remains, in my view, one of the main categories in the study of literature of Mozambique. This essay, I hope, has foregrounded how 'nation' now necessarily signifies in relation to 'world-system' the urgency of turning away from older categories of 'nation', and the importance of this shift for the study of Mozambican literature.

Works cited

Adesokan, Akinwumi. *Postcolonial Artists and Global Aesthetics*. Bloomington: Indiana University Press, 2011.

Al-Rodhan, Nayef R. F., et al. 'Definitions of Globalization: A Comprehensive Overview and a Proposed Definition.' Geneva Centre for Security Policy (2006).

Beecroft, Alexander. *An Ecology of World Literature*. London: Verso, 2015.

Bordwell, David. *Poetics of Cinema*. London and New York: Routledge, 2008.

Brugioni, Elena. 'O outro pé da Sereia: História[s] na Pós-Colonialidade'. *Luso-Brazilian Review* 49, no. 1 (2012): 46–62.

Castells, Manuel. *The Rise of the Network Society*. Oxford: Blackwell Publishing, 1996.

Couto, Mia. *O outro pé da sereia*. Lisbon: Caminho, 2006.

Erlmann, Veit. 'The Aesthetics of the Global Imagination: Reflections on World Music in the 1990s.' *Public Culture*, no. 8 (1996): 467–487.

Fairclough, Norman. *Language and Globalization*. London and New York: Routledge, 2006.

Goodwin, Andrew, and Joe Gore. 'World Beat and the Cultural Imperialism Debate.' *Socialist Review* 20, no. 3 (1990): 63–80.

Guilbault, Jocelyn. *Zouk: World Music in the West Indies*. Chicago and London: University of Chicago Press, 1993.

Gupta, Suman. *Globalization and Literature*. Cambridge: Polity Press, 2006.

Harvey, David. *A Brief History of Neoliberalism*. New York: Oxford University Press, 2005.

Hayot, Eric. *On Literary Worlds*. New York: Oxford University Press, 2012.

Herlinghaus, Hermann. *Narco-Epics: A Global Aesthetics of Sobriety*. New York: Bloomsbury, 2013.

Herwitz, Daniel. *Aesthetics, Arts, and Politics in a Global World*. London and New York: Bloomsbury, 2017.

Iñárritu, Alejandro, and Guillermo Arriaga. *Babel*, DVD, Central Films, Zeta Films, Paramount, 2006.

Jameson, Fredric. *The geopolitical aesthetic: Cinema and space in the world system*. Bloomington: Indiana University Press, 1995.

Jameson, Fredric. 'Notes on Globalization as a Philosophical Issue'. In *The Cultures of Globalization*, Fredric Jameson and Masao Miyoshi. Durham and New York: University of Duke Press, 1998.

Kerr, Paul. '*Babel's* network narrative: packaging a globalised art cinema.' *Transnational Cinemas* 1, no. 1 (2010): 37–51.

Lawall, Sarah. *Reading World Literature: Theory, History, Practice*. Austin: University of Texas Press, 2010.

Liman, John. 'Novel at the Center of the World.' *Electronic Book Review* (2008). Accessed 13 November 2018.

Lopes, João Marques. 'O colonialismo interno em *O Outro Pé da Sereia*, de Mia Couto'. *Letras de Hoje* 51, no. 4 (Oct/Dec 2016): 565–572.

Madureira, Luis. 'Nation, Identity and Loss of Footing: Mia Couto's O Outro Pé Da Sereia and the Question of Lusophone Postcolonialism.' *Novel: A Forum on Fiction 41*, nos. 2–3 (June 2008): 200–28.

Monteiro, Lucineide Rodrigues, and Miguel Nenevé. 'O Outro Pé da Sereia, de Mia Couto: a Desconstrução da Visão Eurocêntrica Sobre Moçambique.' *Polifonia* 19, no. 26 (2012): 52–62.

Newman, Robert. *The Fountain at the Centre of the World*. Brooklyn, NY: Soft Skull Press, 2004.

Russel, David. O., and Jeff Baena. *I Heart Huckabees*, Fox Searchlight Pictures, 2004.

Tutek, Hrvoje. 'The Form of Resistance'. In *Globalizing Literary Genres*, edited by Jernej Habjan and Fabienne Imlinger. London and New York: Routledge, 2015.

Wallerstein, Immanuel. *World-Systems Analysis*. Durham and New York: Duke University Press, 2004.

Werbner, Pnina, ed. *Political Aesthetics of Global Protest: The Arab Spring and Beyond*. Edinburgh: Edinburgh University Press, 2014.

PART II

Mia Couto's Worlds

KAMILA KRAKOWSKA RODRIGUES

5 Literary Ethnographies: The Idea of Nation and Writing Back in *Terra Sonâmbula* and *Macunaíma*

Mia Couto's debut novel, *Terra Sonâmbula (Sleepwalking Land)* was published in 1992, the year of the signing of the Rome General Peace Accords which put an end to the civil war lasting for 16 years. This tragic experience is a central motif of the novel, which opens with the vision of agony of a war-torn Mozambique: 'War had killed the road thereabouts'.[1] This dead road becomes a symbol of the country in ruin, a safe-place and a starting point for an Odyssey of stories, encounters and crossings for the old Tuahir and the orphaned boy Muidinga. Both their physical and imaginary travels and the adventures of Kindzu – the protagonist of the parallel narrative whose deeds are preserved in a collection of notebooks found by Muidinga – incorporate and rewrite various elements of Mozambican oral traditions, local imageries and symbols, many of which were collected and described in Henri Junod's classical ethnographic study *The Life of a South African Tribe* (1912–1913; translated into Portuguese as *Usos e Costumes dos Bantu*).[2] A similar dialogue with ethnographic intertexts can be found in the Brazilian modernist masterpiece *Macunaíma* by Mário de Andrade, which rewrites several ethnographic works, in particular Theodor Koch-Grünberg's *Vom Roraima zum Orinoko* (1911–1913), to construct a rhapsody of an Amerindian (anti-)hero[3] who travels from the Amazon jungle to São Paulo and back,

1 Mia Couto, *Sleepwalking Land* (London: Serpent's Tail, 2006), 1.

2 Henri Junod, *Usos e Costumes dos Bantu. Vol. I* (Maputo: Arquivo Histórico de Moçambique, 1996a); *Usos e Costumes dos Bantu. Vol. II* (Maputo: Arquivo Histórico de Moçambique, 1996b).

3 The representation of Macunaíma as a 'hero without a character' [herói sem nenhum caráter], as stated in the very title of the rhapsody, has been thoroughly discussed by scholars. For a review of different interpretations, see Krakowska Rodrigues, *Na*

inverting the typical trajectories of travel writing.[4] This essay proposes to analyse the role of interweaving those 'ethnographic' passages in the two literary works and the implications of such an interdiscursive practice for constructing a literary idea of a postcolonial nation.

It is important to note that the objective here is by no means to determine how representative those literary works are of extra-linguistic realities. Mia Couto's and Mário de Andrade's texts will be treated as examples of literary ethnographies structured around their own internal logic. Such methodological caveats are in line with the existing body of work on the novels, and especially on *Terra Sonâmbula*. In her seminal work, Fernanda Cavacas adopted a systematic approach to classifying traditional expressions and idioms in Mia Couto's work and determined the origins of his mythical imagery.[5] This research methodology is also present in Manuel Cavalcanti Proença's *Roteiro de Macunaíma* in which the Brazilian scholar traces back the origins of Mário de Andrade's imagery.[6] From a different standpoint, Ana Mafalda Leite (2003) uses the work of Henri Junod to study *Terra Sonâmbula* to 'ilustrar o modo de incorporação múltiplo de intertextos orais, nomeadamente ao nível das formas estruturantes da narrativa' [illustrate the multiple ways of incorporating oral intertexts, namely at the level of narrative structures].[7] Her analysis of genres of oral origin is based on both a comparison with the ethnographic intertext and with common tendencies present in African literatures. In her opinion, narrative proverbs (or stories), proverbs, and parables are narrative units which compose

Demanda da Ideia de Nação. As Viagens Pós-coloniais em Mário de Andrade e Mia Couto (Lisbon: Instituto Camões, 2019).

4 Theodor Koch-Grünberg, *Vom Roroima zum Orinoco. Ergebnisse Einer Reise in Nordbrasilien und Venezuela in den Jahren 1911–1913*. II Band (Stuttgart: Verlag Strecker und Schröder, 1924); Mário de Andrade, *Macunaíma, o herói sem nenhum caráter*, ed. Telê Porto Ancona Lopez (Brasília: CNPq, 1988).

5 Fernanda Cavacas, *Mia Couto: Acrediteísmos* (Lisbon: Mar Além, 2001); *Mia Couto: Pensatempos e Improvérbios* (Lisbon: Mar Além, 2000).

6 Manuel Cavalcanti Proença, *Roteiro de Macunaíma* (São Paulo: Anhembi, 1955).

7 Ana Mafalda Leite, *Literaturas Africanas e Formulações Pós-coloniais* (Lisbon: Colibri, 2003), 45.

Mozambican cultural imagery and have a structuring potential for the foundation of a national literature.[8]

Inspired by those studies among others, Anita Morães addresses methodological issues behind establishing certain parallel lines between literary fiction and ethnographic works, taking as examples precisely the critical reception of *Terra Sonâmbula*, and comparing it to the reception of *Macunaíma*. Moraes identifies a certain expectation of a referential character of fictional texts and warns that the border between reality and fiction becomes diluted in the very process of reading which pretends to 'verify' literary realities.[9] She asks: 'certa literatura africana (como certa literatura brasileira) não vem se produzindo num diálogo e num aproveitamento de materiais etnográficos como matéria prima? Não estaríamos diante de um círculo fechado, de uma espécie de trama discursiva autorreferencial envolvendo etnografia, literatura e crítica literária?' [is a certain African literature (just as a certain Brazilian literature) not being produced in dialogue with and through using ethnographic material as its feedstock? Aren't we confronted with a closed loop, a type of discursive auto-referential weft involving ethnography, literature and literary criticism?].[10] The analysis presented here will follow such precautions in seeking to answer the question of how narratives of ethnographic travels can be used in literary fiction to foster and/or challenge the idea of a nation and construct an 'imagined community' in the context of decolonised countries which need to deconstruct the (frequently Eurocentric) narratives of the past and build their own myths of origins.[11]

Travel narratives, in general, as well as ethnographic writings on both a geographically and a culturally different Other, in particular, need to be understood within the context of knowledge production and its symbiotic

8 Ibid., 58.

9 Anita Martins Rodrigues de Morães, 'Discurso Etnográfico e Representação na Ficção Africana de Língua Portuguesa: Notas sobre a Recepção Crítica de Mia Couto e o Projeto Literário de Ruy Duarte de Carvalho,' *Via Atlântica* 16 (2009): 173–194.

10 Ibid., 182.

11 Benedict Anderson, *Imagined Communities. Reflections on the Origin and Spread of Nationalism* (London: Verso, 1991).

interrelation with power structures, as represented in the Foucauldian power/knowledge concept.[12] While the first decades of the twentieth century brought important changes in the research methodology in ethnography and anthropology (participant observation becoming a golden standard after Malinowski's publication on the Trobriand Islands), the legitimacy of the ethnographer and anthropologist were only put into question in the 1960s.[13] The ethnographic sources the two novels under study use as their inspiration/point of departure were written in a period of unquestioned and unquestionable respect for the ethnographer, described by Clifford as the supposed 'guardian' of the knowledge of/about the Other.[14] The embedding of Koch-Grünberg's and Junod's work in this specific context requires them to be read not only as a valuable collection of local traditions and cultural practices, but also as 'signs of something else', as put forward by Valentin-Ives Mudimbe.[15] In his thought-provoking study, the philosopher proposes to interrogate the 'modalities, significance, or strategies' of discourses on Africa 'as a means of understanding the type of knowledge which is being proposed.'[16]. By incorporating and rewriting the ethnographic publications about their own countries, Mia Couto and much earlier Mário de Andrade precisely engage in this type of creative questioning, a dialogic narrative practice, which Mary Louise Pratt labelled as 'autoethnographic' writing.[17]

Following a story within a story structure, *Terra Sonâmbula* interweaves micro-narratives, many of which incorporate and rewrite elements of local Bantu traditions and mythologies. One of the key symbols which reappears time and again in the novel is the mythical bird mampfana. According to Junod, this bird is a bad sign for the traveller and its appearance is a death

12 Michel Foucault, *Power/Knowledge: Selected Interviews and Other Writings, 1972–1977*, ed. Colin Gordon (Harlow: Pearson Education, 2008).

13 James Clifford, *The Predicament of Culture: Twentieth-Century Ethnography, Literature, and Art*, (Cambridge, Mass.: Harvard Univ. Press, 1988), 21–54.

14 Ibid.

15 Valentin-Yves Mudimbe, *The Invention of Africa*, (London: James Currey, 1988), 9–10.

16 Ibid.

17 Mary Louise Pratt, *Imperial Eyes. Travel Writing and Transculturation*, (London: Routledge, 1992).

warning. Travelers must avoid this creature in order to keep their path 'pure'.[18] In the notebooks composing one of the parallel narratives, 'the bird that kills journeys' appears before Kindzu on his way to the refugees' camp, the last stop in his search for the disappeared son of Farida, a mysterious woman he meets on a sunken ship.[19] His fight against this mythical creature had in fact been foretold by the ghost of his father. The dead man was upset as his passing was not accompanied, in his opinion, by proper traditional ceremonies and did not agree with the plan of his son to set off in a quest to become a naparama warrior and abandon the war. He threatens the boy:

> I would never fulfill any of my dreams as long as his shadow hung over me. The same thing was happening to our whole country, which had divorced itself from its ancestors. The country and I were suffering the same punishment. Then he hurled threats at me: since I wanted this journey so much, the mampfana, the bird that kills journeys, would appear before me one evening. 'It will be perched on top of a huge tree, its wings open,' he said.[20]

As forewarned, the mythical bird stops Kindzu's journey. Kindzu calls his father for help. His father responds and the bird 'was torn in two, severed in half. Its feathers fell out, its talons disintegrated and its body crumbled'.[21] Nonetheless, it is a Pyrrhic victory since the war indeed stops Kindzu's journey and he is killed by the bandits. In those two passages the bird symbolises the war itself, which makes the journeys impossible in both a physical and a metaphorical sense.

Mampfana is a creature whose meaning and existence is intrinsically connected to the notion of free travel and movement. It is a traveller who blocks the paths of others. Its name in the novel is always composed of two elements: the name itself is followed by an epithet, 'the bird that kills journeys'. This descriptive redundancy is typical of oral discourse, but not of the mythical context in which it seems to appear in Couto's novel. Many animals, especially those considered dangerous by totemic societies, are subject to linguistic taboos. Their names should not be pronounced for

18 Junod, *Usos e Costumes dos Bantu. Vol. I*, 310.
19 Couto, *Sleepwalking Land*, 189.
20 Ibid., 40.
21 Ibid., 189.

fear that the animals, or rather the divinity which they represent, might respond to the calling, and therefore synonyms and paraphrases are created.[22] However, Mia Couto uses systematically both the 'true' name and the descriptive phrase. This evocation of the same concept using two signifiers can have a double function. On the one hand, this epithet can be interpreted as a 'para-definition' of the term, explaining its meaning to the readers not familiar with Tsonga mythology. However, the same objective could have been achieved with a footnote or a glossary. On the other hand, this redundant expression can be read as complementary to the name, highlighting the destructive power of the bird. Thus, as a 'bird that kills journeys', mampfana becomes a metaphor for the war itself.

Can such incorporation of elements of local traditions be an attempt to bridge the gap between Mozambican cultures through intercultural translation? Do *Terra Sonâmbula*'s characters play the role of travellers-translators? According to Michael Cronin, every traveller necessarily engages in the translation process at different levels throughout their travel experience. They translate between languages, but also between different semiotic systems, which involves contextualisation of the culture of the 'Other', but also can lead to the rethinking of the traveller's own culture.[23] Kindzu's travels seem to be a unique opportunity to reflect on different cultural experiences and encounters, but also create the need to come to terms with his ambiguous position as both insider and outsider in this cultural landscape. In the case of the Brazilian rhapsody, Mário de Andrade openly reflects upon his position as an author/ethnographer in the preface to *Macunaíma*. He refuses to allow the book to be taken as a folklore study or as a source of documentation of customs and traditions. However, he does not only incorporate ethnographic studies by authors such as Karl von den Steinen or Barbosa Rodrigues, but also himself adopts the position of an ethnographer apprentice researching macumba customs in Rio de Janeiro to complete one of the chapters of the novel. As described in the unpublished notes to the preface, the interaction with the people

22 Murray Barnson Emeneau, 'Taboos on Animal Names,' *Language* 24, no. 1 (Jan–Mar 1948): 56–63.

23 Michael Cronin, *Across the Lines: Travel, Language, Translation* (Cork: Cork University Press, 2000), 2.

involved in the ritual, who become his 'local informants', was crucial in this process.[24] However, Andrade stresses that those elements are merged with pure literary fiction. Crossing the borders between academic research and literary fiction, between notions of home and abroad, Andrade creates his own literary (auto-)ethnography – returning to the concept of Mary Louise Pratt – which enters into dialogue with Eurocentric representations of Brazil in travel narratives in general (e.g. the parody of Pero Vaz de Caminha's letter to King Manuel I of Portugal), but also destabilises the foundations of ethnographic discourse and questions its legitimacy.[25]

Terra Sonâmbula does not include a passage with a clear paratextual reflection on the incorporation of such ethnographic elements, but there are several episodes which point to a critical rethinking of the possibilities and the limits of knowing the Other and its culture, even within the borders of an imagined national community. In this context, the meeting of the orphaned and traumatised Muidinga (in the overarching narrative plot in *Terra Sonâmbula*) with the scurrilous old ladies is very meaningful. Wandering around the deserted roundabouts of the burnt bus, the boy reaches a plot of cultivated land. There he spots a group of women chanting and hitting the ground with sticks. Muidinga is initially very curious and excited about this unexpected encounter. However, his longing for contact with other human beings rapidly transforms into fear when he is surrounded by women who start beating him with sticks and throwing sand and stones at him. An attack of a group of women against a man who crosses their path during a sacred ceremony is clearly inspired by the ritual of the *nunu*, a little beetle devastating the corn and bean crops in the coastal area of Baía da Lagoa. This custom is described in detail by Henri Junod.[26] However, Mia Couto does not incorporate all the elements constitutive of this ritual and ignores, for example, the crucial role of a twin woman, who has sole responsibility for throwing the collected beetles into the closest lagoon. Instead of presenting the custom in every detail, adopting the perspective

24 Mário de Andrade, 'Prefácio a *Macunaíma*', (1928). In *Macunaíma: A Margem e o Texto*, ed. Telê Porto Ancona Lopez (São Paulo: HUCITEC, 1974), 90–94.

25 Mary Louise Pratt, *Imperial Eyes*.

26 Junod, *Usos e Costumes dos Bantu. Vol. II*, 377–378.

of a narrator-ethnographer, the writers chooses to focus on the emotions and feelings of Muidinga.

The boy clearly does not understand the reasons behind the behaviour of the elderly women. After the attack, he asks 'What happened?' and Tuahir explains to him 'in a fatherly way' the meaning of the ritual.[27] Besides cultural differences, a linguistic frontier also separates the boy from the old women. As highlighted many times along the narrative, the women shout at Muidinga 'in a language he can't understand' and on the other hand the women also cannot understand the boy's desperate question: 'Why are you hitting me, mothers?'[28] Such linguistic barriers, as well as the lack of a common cultural background illustrated in this episode, seem to question the utopian idea that travel narratives can represent the Other and foster the opportunities for a fluid intercultural communication.

The Mozambique that is portrayed in *Terra Sonâmbula* is a multicultural country that is still in the process of becoming acquainted with itself. However, the first step to form Mozambican identity is not simply to collect and describe the customs and traditions of its peoples, but rather to acknowledge that difference exists. This step is crucial given Mozambique's post-independence history during which the FRELIMO government implemented several unification policies, which aimed at avoiding tribal conflicts in the newly born nation, but were implemented in a very rigid and authoritarian way, discouraging local cultural expressions, among other consequences.[29] In the novel, the various myths and rituals of different ethnic groups are combined in a literary narrative without referencing their ethnic or regional origins. Just as in the 'degeographised' Brazil of *Macunaíma*, which rewrites the deeds of three native Indian legendary characters – Macunaíma, Kalawunseg and Kunevo[30] – the ethnographic

27 Couto, *Sleepwalking Land*, 102.

28 Ibid., 101.

29 See Carlos Serra, *Novos Combates pela Mente Sociológica. Sociologia Política das Relações de Poder em Moçambique* (Maputo: Livraria Universitária da Universidade Eduardo Mondlane, 1997); Phillip Rothwell, *A Postmodern Nationalist: Truth, Orality and Gender in the Work of Mia Couto* (Lewisburg: Bucknell University Press, 2004).

30 Proença, *Roteiro de Macunaíma*.

micro-narratives in *Terra Sonâmbula* set the stage for a reflection on the mechanism behind the auto-representation and identity formation processes in highly multicultural and decentred nations. Both novels compose a literary ethnography, apparently with no clear origins, which can contribute to the self-invention of Mozambique and Brazil as imagined communities.

However, as myths and legends from particular local cultures are incorporated within the narrative of the nation in both *Macunaíma* and *Terra Sonâmbula*, their role is also put into question. The episode of the scurrilous old ladies seems to point to the fact that the nation needs multiple stories, multiple narratives to foster the ties of belonging between various groups that form this nation. Muidinga is not able to understand the behaviour of the elderly women who attack him, but the old Tuahir manages to bring different communities closer together by telling the story of the *nunu* hunting and, therefore, sharing their cultural background. Such a bidirectional movement between contributing to and challenging national myth-making can be found in *Macunaíma* in the episode in which the hero retells the myth of Pauí-Pódole at a square in São Paulo. The hero is enraged by hearing an account of the Southern Cross constellation as a symbol of Brazilian national identity and decides to intervene and tell the 'true' story in which he identifies the four stars as Pauí-Pódole, or Father of Mutum. His discourse reproduces almost word by word the legend of the Arelunà Akuli tribe as registered by Theodor Koch-Grünberg.[31] According to the legend, Pauí-Pódole is resting on top of a tree when he is discovered by two companions who decide to hunt him. After many adventures, Pauí-Pódole decides to fly to the sky where he will not be bothered anymore and transforms himself into a constellation.

31 'Pauí-pódole flog zum Himmel und wurde dort in ein Sternbild verwandelt. Kamayuá flog hinter ihm her, um ihn mit dem Blasrohr zuschießen. Auch sie wurde in einen Stern verwandelt. Es kam auch Kunowá mith einem Feuerbrand in der Hand, um Kamayuá den Weg zu beleuchten. Auch sie flog bis zum Himmel und blieb dort als Stern zwischen Pauí-pódole und Kamayuá' [Pauí-Pódole flew to the sky and transformed himself into a constellation. Kamayuá chased him to shoot him down with a blowpipe. And he also got transformed into a star. Then there came also Kunowá with a torch in his hand, to illuminate Kamayuá's way. He also flew to the sky and became a star between Pauí-Pódole and Kamayuá] (Koch-Grünberg, *Vom Roroima zum Orinoco*, 63).

However, this celestial ending is presented by Mário de Andrade within the aesthetic of surrealism and the absurd. The torch which illuminates the way to the sky is held by thousands of people, families, generations, civil servants, and even the chief of the police, the long enumeration creating a hyperbolic image of unity and collaboration. This shift between the sublime and the profane, between a dissemination of a myth and its deconstruction is even more visible in the account of the reaction of the crowd gathered at the square, in which the sensation of universal fraternity and shared beliefs is immediately contrasted with the image of those people returning to their homes drunk and urinating in bed. Those contrasting images do not point to the existence (or literary creation) of a symbolic bond between the Brazilian North and South, between the forests of Uraricoera and the urban landscape of São Paulo, but rather question the possibilities of forming an imagined community within a country of extremely high social, cultural and economic diversity.

Such a (de)constructive rewriting of oral myths, traditions and beliefs recollected and described by European ethnographers in the second decade of the twentieth century calls forth a reflection on the very process of nation-building in the postcolonial reality. Although *Macunaíma* clearly reflects the modernist tendencies of its time[32] and predates the academic debates on 'othering' in ethnographic and anthropological studies, it engages the reader in a complex process of looking at oral traditions not as canonical texts for defining the essence of the (re)discovered national identity, but rather as texts-in-process, performed time and again, reinterpreted, misinterpreted or even completely forgotten in a constant play of identity building. Indeed, *Macunaíma* does not represent a 'synthesis'

32 It is important to note that although Mário de Andrade never took part in the Anthropophagic Movement, his rhapsody was to be the first text to be published in the 'Anthropophagic Library' series. In fact, the writer complains in a letter to Alceu Amoroso Lima about the coincidence of his rhapsody being published at the same time as Oswaldo de Andrade's Manifesto, but decides to collaborate 'because it is a friends' initiative' [por causa de ser feita por amigos] (Andrade, *Macunaíma*, 400). Both texts can be thus seen as a playful vanguard response to the urgency of rethinking Brazilian identity that, according to Sirlei Silveira, had been at the very centre of intellectual debates since independence; see Sirlei Silveira, *O Brasil de Mário de Andrade* (Campo Grande, MS: Ed. UFMS, 1999), 21.

of Brazil, as Mário de Andrade openly states in his foreword, but rather plays with pieces and fragments that together, in different constellations and arrangements, represent the idea of the nation not as a stable referent but as a process of 'being and becoming'. Interestingly, *Terra Sonâmbula*, although written in the early 1990s, in a different socio-economic and political context, invites the reader to the same epistemological exercise of interpreting different layers of intertexts and asking how we construct and imagine our identities. In his classical study, Phillip Rothwell argues that the appeal of Mia Couto's work lies in his ability to bridge 'the apparent opposition between nationalism's need for a border, and postmodernism's dissolution of all frontiers'.[33] The incorporation of ethnographic accounts of local customs and traditions seems to open up narrative interstices, liminal spaces where a border is depicted as a porous, fractal structure embodying both voices and silences that form the textual weft of the Mozambican imagined community.

In conclusion, both Mário de Andrade and Mia Couto use ethnographic intertexts as an inspiration to create literary realities, which seem to stress the importance of the very act of narrating as crucial for the formation of an idea of a nation. Literature is here not a mirror of customs and traditions as documented by European scientists, but rather a space for reflection on the legitimacy of a traveller to represent the Other and on the role of shared myths in creating ties of relation in the imagined communities of multicultural nations like those of Brazil and Mozambique. Misunderstandings, communication flaws, intercultural tensions are core elements of their literary ethnographies which cherish national diversity, but also acknowledge the socio-political threats that diversity might create. However, literary narratives may become productive spaces in which the 'barred Nation It/Self, alienated from its eternal self-generation, becomes a liminal signifying space that is internally marked by the discourses of minorities, the heterogeneous histories of contending peoples, antagonistic authorities and tense locations of cultural difference.'[34] Mia Couto's

33 Phillip Rothwell, *A Postmodern Nationalist. Truth, Orality, and Gender in the Work of Mia Couto* (Lewisburg: Bucknell University Press, 2004), 16.

34 Homi Bhabha, *The Location of Culture* (London: Routledge, 1994), 212.

words on the reception of his work in Mozambique reflect precisely such frictions in the process of narrating the nation:

> People invent themselves and, when they invent themselves, they perform this double function of creating a nation, of creating part of the nation and also of creating Mozambican literature. I think it's something fortuitous that's happening here in Mozambique because that idea of the nation is not yet fully grounded – as a type of frame around all identities – people have this opportunity to do extraordinary things, and it's always correct. It's always correct within the limits of a sensibility that has been determined in terms of power. Insofar as it is fiction, it doesn't disturb.[35]

Works cited

Anderson, Benedict. *Imagined Communities. Reflections on the Origin and Spread of Nationalism*. London: Verso, 1991.

Andrade, Mário de. *Macunaíma, o herói sem nenhum caráter*. Edited by Telê Porto Ancona Lopez. Brasília: CNPq, 1988.

Andrade, Mário de. 'Prefácio a *Macunaíma*' (1928). In *Macunaíma: A Margem e o Texto*, edited by Telê Porto Ancona Lopez, 90–94. São Paulo: HUCITEC, 1974.

Bhabha, Homi. *The Location of Culture*. London: Routledge, 1994.

Cavacas, Fernanda. *Mia Couto: Acrediteísmos*. Lisbon: Mar Além, 2001.

Cavacas, Fernanda. *Mia Couto: Pensatempos e Improvérbios*. Lisbon: Mar Além, 2000.

Cavalcanti Proença, Manuel. *Roteiro de Macunaíma*. São Paulo: Anhembi, 1955.

Clifford, James. *The Predicament of Culture: Twentieth-Century Ethnography, Literature, and Art*. Cambridge, Mass.: Harvard University Press, 1988.

Couto, Mia. *Sleepwalking Land*. London: Serpent's Tail, 2006.

Couto, Mia. Interview. In *Speaking the Postcolonial Nation. Voices from Angola and Mozambique*, edited by Ana Mafalda Leite et al., 173–198. Oxford: Peter Lang, 2014.

Cronin, Michael. *Across the Lines: Travel, Language, Translation*. Cork: Cork University Press, 2000.

35 Mia Couto, Interview, in *Speaking the Postcolonial Nation. Voices from Angola and Mozambique*, ed. Ana Mafalda Leite et al. (Oxford: Peter Lang, 2014), 173–198.

Emeneau, Murray Barnson. 'Taboos on Animal Names'. *Language* 24, no. 1 (Jan–Mar 1948): 56–63.

Foucault, Michel. *Power/Knowledge: Selected Interviews and Other Writings, 1972–1977*. Edited by Colin Gordon. Harlow: Pearson Education, 2008.

Hall, Stuart. 'Cultural Identity and Diaspora'. In Stuart Hall, *Identity: Community, Culture, Difference*, edited by Jonathan Rutherford, 222–237. London: Lawrence and Wishart, 1990.

Junod, Henri. *Usos e Costumes dos Bantu. Vol. I*. Maputo: Arquivo Histórico de Moçambique, 1996a.

Junod, Henri. *Usos e Costumes dos Bantu. Vol. II*. Maputo: Arquivo Histórico de Moçambique, 1996b.

Koch-Grünberg, Theodor. *Vom Roroima zum Orinoco. Ergebnisse Einer Reise in Nordbrasilien und Venezuela in den Jahren 1911–1913*. II Band. Stuttgart: Verlag Strecker und Schröder, 1924.

Leite, Ana Mafalda. *Literaturas Africanas e Formulações Pós-coloniais*. Lisbon: Colibri, 2003.

Morães, Anita Martins Rodrigues de. 'Discurso Etnográfico e Representação na Ficção Africana de Língua Portuguesa: Notas Sobre a Recepção Crítica de Mia Couto e o Projeto Literário de Ruy Duarte de Carvalho.' *Via Atlântica* 16 (2009): 173–194.

Mudimbe, Valentin-Yves. *The Invention of Africa*. London: James Currey, 1988.

Pratt, Mary Louise. *Imperial Eyes. Travel Writing and Transculturation*. London: Routledge, 1992.

Rothwell, Philip. *A Postmodern Nationalist: Truth, Orality and Gender in the Work of Mia Couto*. Lewisburg: Bucknell University Press, 2004.

Serra, Carlos. *Novos Combates pela Mente Sociológica. Sociologia Política das Relações de Poder em Moçambique*. Maputo: Livraria Universitária da Universidade Eduardo Mondlane, 1997.

IRENE MARQUES

6 Female Resistance and Engagement in Combating Intersecting Powers of Colonialisms and Patriarchies in Mia Couto's *Woman of the Ashes*

The present study explores how the historical novel *Mulheres de Cinza* (2015)/*Woman of the Ashes* (2018) by Mia Couto (Mozambique) gives voice to women by portraying them as active agents fighting multiple and intersecting powers pertaining to European and African colonialisms and patriarchies, ethnicity, class and race.[1] Dealing with the wars of resistance against Portuguese colonialism and the VaNguni occupations led by the powerful African Emperor Ngungunyane in Mozambique at the end of the nineteenth century, *Woman of the Ashes*, the first book of a trilogy depicting the end of Ngungunyane's empire and the victory of Portuguese colonial power over the Gaza region, presents to us a complex and multifaceted narrative where the female voice, through one of the main narrating characters (Imani, a VaChopi girl), occupies a central position serving multiple purposes: as a carrier of ancestral voice (in terms of history, culture and orature), and critic and resister of Portuguese and Mozambican patriarchies, and Portuguese and VaNguni colonialisms. My analysis addresses important issues related to different types of 'feminisms' and 'patriarchies' (related to Africa and Europe), intersectionalities of gender, race, class, ethnicity and colonialism, wars of resistance, and the importance of African women in combating colonialism. The latter aspect is important given women's frequent absence from what have been mostly patriarchal historical accounts of wars of resistance and independence

1 Couto *Woman of the Ashes*, trans. David Brookshaw (New York: Farrar, Straus and Giroux, 2018); Mia Couto, *Mulheres de Cinza* (Lisbon: Editorial Caminho, 2015).

on the African continent, which have tended to neglect women's key contributions. Such trend has been common not only in Mozambique but also in other countries such as Algeria, South Africa, Kenya and Zimbabwe,[2] where women also had major roles in direct and indirect combat against colonial domination. In that sense, these two novels are the very site where history is corrected or added to, thus creating a more balanced account of history.

Woman of the Ashes alternates between the voice of Imani, a 15-year-old VaChopi girl from the village of Nkokolani in the interior of Mozambique, and Germano de Melo, the Portuguese Sergeant sent to Mozambique to defend and assert Portuguese power and interests in the region. The novel takes place at the end of the nineteenth century when direct European colonialism is entrenching itself all over Africa through political and administrative institutions to put in practice the goals set out in the 1884–5 Berlin conference, which required effective occupation by the different colonial powers. At the time, the Portuguese presence in Mozambique was still in many ways peripheral. There were territorial disputes with the English and local African groups and the Portuguese needed to gain control over the areas occupied by the VaNguni, whose leader was the mighty Ngungunyane

2 For important discussions on women's roles in independence battles and colonial resistance in different African countries, see E. E. Kombo, 'Women in National Liberation Wars in the Settler Colonies of Kenya and Zimbabwe: Pathways to Political Empowerment' (M.A. by Research, University of York, 2012), <https://muse.jhu.edu/article/558536/pdf;> and Tanya Lyons and Mark Israel, 'Women, Resistance and the Armed Struggle in Southern Africa,' in *African Identities: Contemporary Political and Social Challenges* (*Making of Modern Africa*) ed. Abebe Zegeye and Paul Ahluwalia (New York: Routledge, 2018). Algerian women participated in the war of independence in many different and important ways. As seen in the 1966 film *The Battle of Algiers* and argued by Meredeth Turshen (in 'Algerian Women in the Liberation Struggle and the Civil War: From Active Participants to Passive Victims,' *Social Research: An International Quarterly* 69, no. 3 (2002): 889–91. <https://muse.jhu.edu/>) women served as combatants, bomb carriers, spies, fundraisers, couriers, nurses, launderers, cooks, etc. However, it is important to note that women's roles were mostly of a supportive and indirect nature and less in direct combat – which, however, did not make them any less important.

(or Gungunhane/Gungunhana as the Portuguese called him).[3] De Melo was promised an army of Portuguese soldiers with an Angolan platoon to follow soon after him to aid in the colonial enterprise, but they never came, leaving him largely alone to assert colonial power in the area – indicating that Portuguese occupation and effective control of the Mozambican colony was scanty at the time and mostly relegated to coastal areas.

The VaChopi are, on the surface at least and initially, on the side of the Portuguese as they also see themselves as victims of Gungunhane's violent empire and are fighting against him and his attempts to take over their territories. They are, we can argue, in the midst of two colonial powers and often unsure which of two devils is worse, even though, as is evident in the novel in many ways, the racist ideologies of the Portuguese empire are present in different forms and Africans are frequently depicted as inferior others who need to be civilised. This is one of the main reasons why, throughout the novel, we see some characters switching allegiance and joining the VaNguni (and in particular Imani's brother Dunbula) or at the very least questioning the motives of the Portuguese and going against their directives.

Imani is quite aware of the fact that she is being colonised and oppressed by the Portuguese on many levels, even if she starts off by being on their side and serves at the interpreter for Germano de Melo, her family being the only one in the area who has (on the surface) assimilated into the Portuguese culture, speaking the Portuguese language and adhering to Christianity – and for that very reason, seen with suspicion by the other VaChopi who see them as sell-outs to the Portuguese and traitors to their race and culture in many ways.

Although the narrative alternates between Imani and Germano, the former occupies a more central role in the novel. The narrative opens with Imani's voice and she serves as the gateway to the other women of the family, like her grandmother, mother, and to all the other characters in the novel, such as her brothers, father, grandfather and ancestors – giving us a window into the complexity of the VaChopi world, their history, the

3 Malyn Newitt, *A History of Mozambique* (London: Hurst & Company, 1995), 293–297, 317–355.

wars with the VaNguni and the Portuguese, and religious and cultural practices – often by recalling stories passed on to her, thus making oral tradition a central aspect of this novel. The oral tradition is in fact a trademark of Couto's overall writing, a literary technique that serves to honour African/Mozambican modes of storytelling, cultural traditions and modes of representation. Commenting on the importance of orality in his writing, Couto has said the following:

> The most important influences on my writing come from those I can't identify, persons that populated my childhood, my hometown in the Indian Ocean, the neighbourhood where I was born and where I started to dream about other places and other lives. So, ironically, the main source of inspiration of my writing came from the non-writing world.[4]

Speaking about *Woman of the Ashes* (and the other books of the trilogy), Couto noted that an important objective of this trilogy is to add versions of the truth to the historical versions that have been published about Gungunhane's life and deeds, either by the Portuguese colonists or in the postcolonial Mozambican narratives of nation-building, arguing that both offer inadequate accounts.[5] If Portuguese colonial historical accounts tend to minimise Gungunhane's power and aggrandise the role of Mouzinho de Albuquerque, who defeated him, post-independence Mozambican nationalist narratives have also tended to aggrandise and idealise him, transforming him into an African hero and overlooking the violence of his empire towards other African ethnic groups. Couto has commented on this when speaking about his novel *O outro pé da sereia*:[6]

> One of the ideas that run through this book [*O outro pé da sereia*] is that we must revisit history from another perspective, one that interrogates and questions the

4 Mia Couto, interview by Scott Esposito, 'We Are Made of Memories: A Conversation with Mia Couto', *The Paris Review*, May 2, 2013, <http://www.theparisreview.org/blog/2013/05/02/we-are-made-of-memories-a-conversation-with-mia-couto/>.

5 Mia Couto, 'Mia Couto, Fnac Chiado, 20/10/2015. Apresentação do seu novo livro Mulheres de Cinza', *You Tube*, <https://www.youtube.com/watch?v=gNqFz2aZnGQ> and 'Mia Couto: *Mulheres de Cinza*', *You Tube*, <https://www.youtube.com/watch?v=CCgOjEjLHsI>.

6 Mia Couto, *O outro pé da sereia* (Lisbon: Editorial Caminho, 2006).

> constructions and mystifications that we have made about our own history because our history is a dangerously mystified one. I know that the founding myths of nations have to be there and we cannot interrogate them from a rigorous historical prism, but those myths of ours serve to, on one hand, construct the nation, and at the same time are being used by a certain elite who wants to erase critical opinions. Deep down, today's elite is prolonging what had been the role of preceding elites and those elites were accomplices in many things though today there is this idea that Africans were all victims, that none were guilty and that is something that immobilises and paralyses us.[7]

Commenting on the tendency to create historical narratives that are false or inaccurate and that promote dichotomous ideas of losers and winners, the late and renowned Kenyan scholar Ali A. Mazrui has noted in 'Cultural Amnesia, Cultural Nostalgia and False Memory: Africa's Identity Crisis Revisited':

> [I]n the broader and historical context of the encounters between Africans and Europeans – the role of collective memory [has] four functions of preservation, selection, elimination and invention. [P]ositive preservation of memory can become a form of *nostalgia* and negative selection by memory can lead to elimination and *amnesia*. [B]oth nostalgia and amnesia can be forms of 'getting one's history wrong' in order to get one's national identity right. [Moreover] historical invention can be consolidated into a false memory – placing something in the past which was never there before.[8]

Moving more directly to the main objectives of this paper, let me now address some of the different ways in which *Woman of the Ashes*, through the narration of Imani, serves as a carrier of ancestral voice and VaChopi culture that privilege women's speech, offer a critique of Portuguese and Mozambican patriarchies and also resist both Portuguese and VaNguni colonialisms. The fact that the novel is called *Woman of the Ashes* is already an indication of women's centrality in Couto's narrative: he wants to give voice, story and history to the women who have been silenced by history or other cultural and ideological mechanisms which have suppressed

7 Mia Couto, quoted in, Elena Brugioni, 'O outro pé da sereia: História[s] na pós-colonialidade,' *Luso-Brazilian Review* 49, no. 1 (2012), 51 (my translation).

8 Ali A. Mazrui, 'Cultural Amnesia, Cultural Nostalgia and False Memory: Africa's Identity Crisis Revisited,' *African and Asian Studies* 12, issues 1–2 (2013), 13.

their rights and prevented them from fully realising their humanity. From the ashes they will rise, as it were.[9] The epigraph placed at the beginning of the first chapter further signals the importance of the female voice. It reads: 'Mother says: Life is made like string. We need to braid it until we can no longer distinguish its threads from our fingers'[10]. The Mother figure here does not refer to Imani's own biological mother (at least not directly) but rather to the Mother creator, the powerful energy that gave life to all and everything. This epigraph further suggests a holistic way of understanding life typical of pre-colonial Mozambique: all and everything is interrelated, which is why it is said, 'We need to braid it [Life] until we can no longer distinguish its threads from our fingers.'[11] Human beings and nature, visible and invisible realities, and the living and the dead (the ancestors) are all intertwined, part of a whole. This relational and holistic ontological view of life is present in the novel in numerous other ways and is another important trademark of Couto's writing – a writing that frequently aims to uphold African systems of thought.[12] As Imani notes:

9 See Ungulani Ba Ka Khosa's books, *Ualalapi* (Lisbon: Editorial Camhino, 1987) and *Gungunhana* (Porto: Porto Editora, 2018). *Ualalapi*, and its second edition *Gungunhana*, which has an added section titled 'As mulheres do imperador', are also fictional historical accounts surrounding the life of Gungunhana that question history and the myth of grandeur about Gungunhana. Moreover, this second edition with the added section titled 'As mulheres do imperador' also intends to bring women to the centre of the narration by giving them voice and centrality in the narrative.

10 Couto, *Woman of the Ashes*, 3.

11 Ibid. 3.

12 I have written extensively on how Couto's fiction frequently recreates holistic and relational ways of life common in pre-colonial (and also colonial and postcolonial) Mozambique and how orality and poetic language are an integral part of his literary enterprise. I have also argued that this way of life shares traits with Buddhist philosophy and even some of the ideologies put forward in the philosophy of Emmanuel Lévinas and Luce Irigaray. See, Irene Marques, 'Spaces of Magic: Couto's Relational Practices', in *A Companion to Mia Couto*, ed. Grant Hamilton and David Huddart (Suffolk: James Currey, 2017), 64–85*; and* 'Suspending the "Lack" Through Art: African and Western Epistemological and Artistic Intersections (Mia Couto, Wole Soyinka, Léopold Senghor, Gaston Bachelard and Mark Epstein)', African Studies 27, issue 1 (2018), 127–142; 'The Way/s of "Poetry": The Contracting and Expanding Self in the Writing of Mia Couto', *JALA: Journal of the African Literature*

> The Portuguese don't understand why we take such care to sweep around the outside of our houses. As far as they are concerned, it makes sense to sweep only inside buildings. It never occurs to them to take a broom to the loose sand in the backyard. Europeans don't understand: For us, what's outside is still inside. The house isn't the building. It's the place that is blessed by the dead, inhabitants who ignore doors and walls.[13]

This relational way of being and seeing, which I have termed 'metaphors of junction' in my other work on Mia Couto,[14] is present throughout the novel in many different ways. The very ending of the novel reiterates that as Imani sees herself spread in the vastness of the land, in the waters of rivers and oceans, her body is no longer a single entity, but rather an immensity that encompasses the entire reality:

> It is strange how our farewells shrink the size of time. My fifteen years pass by me in a flash. My mother's body is now that of a child. And it grows smaller and smaller, until it is no bigger than a fruit. And she tells me: *Before you were born, before you first saw the light of day, you had known rivers and oceans*. And something within me is torn apart, as if I know that I shall never go back to Nkokolani.[15]

The individual self now becomes a collective self that includes the living and the dead, the visible and invisible, the human and the non-human,

Association, Vol. 9, No. 2 (Summer/Fall 2015), 75–111; and *Transcultural Discourses on Class, Gender, and Cultural Identity* (West Lafayette: Purdue University Press, 2011), Chapter 1.

13 Couto, *Woman of the Ashes*, 8.

14 For other discussions about the role of water in Couto's early fiction, see Phillip Rothwell, 'Seaing into the Unconscious: The Role of Water in Mia Couto', *A Postmodern Nationalist: Truth, Orality, and Gender in the Work of Mia Couto* (Lewisburg: Bucknell University Press, 2004), 91–132.

Rothwell points out that water is a way to 'sea' (see) into the unconscious. I add that access to the unconscious is a way to rescue pre-colonial values that have been repressed with Portuguese colonisation. See my discussions on this in *Transcultural Discourses on Class, Gender, and Cultural Identity*, West Lafayette: Purdue University Press (2011), Chapter 1. For discussions on pre-colonial African epistemologies and ontologies, see Teffo J. Lebisa and Abraham P. J. Roux, 'Themes in African Metaphysics', and Didier N. Kaphagawani and Jeanette G. Malherbe, 'African Epistemology', in *The African Philosophy Reader*, ed. P. H. Coetzee and A. P. J. Roux (New York: Routledge, 2003), 161–174 and 219–230.

15 Couto, *Woman of the Ashes*, 54.

all life-force. Water, an element that appears constantly in the novel, is associated with the place where all life-force resides – a fluid element that 'breaks' Imani's self, making her part of a collective whole. Imani becomes like water herself, malleable and able to merge with everything and everyone, allowing others and otherness to enter her, receiving all that exists in her single body/self. She is, in a sense, always becoming. The last chapter of the novel is in fact called 'A Road Made of Water', conjuring again that idea of a self beyond the individual – or a self that only fulfils its ontological destiny (matures) once it recognises itself as part of a vast chain of beings (dead and alive, visible and invisible, human and non-human). Time itself is shrunk and Imani becomes 'old' in the sense that she recognises herself as being part of (entangled in, as it were) a vast chain of beings, thus inhabiting what we may call an unbroken time and universal beingness. When her mother says to her that '*Before [she was] born, before [she] first saw the light of day, [she] had known rivers and oceans*', she means precisely that Imani's existence preceded her birth because she was already connected (inhabiting) the collective chain of beings/beingness.

The first chapter, narrated by Imani, opens with a story of creation about the land of the VaChopi, pointing to the importance of rescuing the VaChopi culture and religion in the narrative. The story of creation, told to Imani by her own mother, signalling the importance of women in transmitting culture and history, tells us of a place that had been whole and perfect in the past, when people had their own names and spoke their own language, before being conquered first by the Portuguese and then by Gungunhane. These conquests shattered the world order, creating chaos and identity crisis:

> Each morning, seven suns would rise over the plains of Inharrime. In those times, the firmament was much larger, and all the stars were contained within it, the living and the dead. Naked just as she had slept, our mother would leave the house, a sieve in her hand. She was going to choose the best of the suns. With her sieve, she would gather up the remaining six stars and bring them back to the village. She would bury them next to the anthill behind our house. That was our graveyard for heavenly creatures. One day, if we ever needed to, we would go and unearth stars. With such a bequest, we were not poor. That's what our mother, Chikazi Makwakwa, said. Or just *mame*, in our native language. Whoever visited us would be aware of the other reason for this belief. It was in the anthill that we buried the placentas of newborn

> babies. A mafura tree had taken root on top of it. We would tie white cloths around its trunk. It was there that we talked to our dead. But the anthill was the opposite of a cemetery. It was a guardian of the rains, and within it dwelt our eternity.[16]
>
> One day, when the morning had been well sieved, a boot trampled on the sun, the sun that Mother had chosen. It was a military boot, like those worn by the Portuguese. This time, however, it was worn by an Nguni soldier. The soldier had been sent by the emperor Ngungunyane. Emperors hunger for land, and their soldiers are mouths that devour nations. That boot shattered the sun into a thousand pieces. And the day turned to darkness. All the other days as well. The seven suns were dying under the soldiers' boots. Our land was being gobbled up. Devoid of stars to nourish our dreams, we learned to be poor. And we lost our eternity too. Knowing that eternity is merely another name for life.[17]

When taking the territory by force, both colonisers impose a new language and new customs oppressing the VaChopi physically and psychologically, making them live in fear and alienated from themselves. They lose their 'eternity' because they don't have access to the anthill where the five suns and the placentas of dead babies are buried. The 'dead' of the anthill (placentas and the suns) represent access to the invisible world, all the dead, revealing the deep link between the world of the living and the world of the dead and all that exists, referred to as 'eternity'. 'Eternity' is Life, full life, holistic, relational life.

Throughout the novel we find many other examples of how Imani and other women perceive the shattering of the initial world order through the violence that came with both colonisers: the Portuguese and the VaNguni. They destroy the land, rape the women and have little respect for anything, only worshiping power. The war is also always or mostly associated with men: they are the ones who continuously engage in it as if they have a destructive seed inside them pulling them towards annihilation – their own and that of others and especially women, depriving the world of its feminine element: '*It was men in uniform that raped women in this village*. This is what men did in obedience to the orders of war. They created a world without mothers, sisters, daughters. War required such world, deprived of women, in order to survive.'[18] War is masculine: it destroys women and

16 Ibid., 3.
17 Ibid., 7–8.
18 Ibid., 220.

therefore life since women are the givers of life. The epigraph to Chapter 5 reiterates how detrimental wars are and equates humans with violence and animals with goodness: 'Lucky are those who, having forsaken their humanity, become creatures of the wild. Unlucky are those who kill on the orders of others, and even more unlucky those who kill on the orders of no one at all. Finally, wretched are those who, having killed, look at themselves in the mirror and still believe they are people.'[19] Men lose their humanity with war and cease to be beings worthy of respect. Imani even thinks that it might be good if Gungunhana takes her as a wife, which would allow her to bring peace to the nations: 'I would, at long last, be a woman. I would finally be a mother. And, as a queen and a mother, I would have power over the VaNguni. And I would bring peace to our nations. My brothers would return home; my sisters would live again; my mother would stop wandering through the darkness in her sleep.'[20]

Both the VaChopi and Portuguese patriarchies are attacked and critically reflected upon by Imani and other women in the novel. Imani is aware that VaChopi women carry many burdens and that men have much more privilege. For instance, even if men are seen as the ones responsible for lighting fire, women in fact do the work but take no credit, as Imani notes ironically in the following passage: 'Following the example of the other wives in Nkokolani, my mother had left large bundles of firewood burning during the night. That was what they always did. In the morning, when the houses awoke once more, the fire was already lit. In this way, the men were spared the task of lighting a new fire. In our village, lighting a flame is the exclusive responsibility of husbands.'[21] In the VaChopi tradition women are also expected to marry and give birth to children, while not marrying by a certain age is seen as problematic. Women exist (become) through community. As single entities they hold little value: it is their attachment to a family (husband, children or extended family) that makes them BE:

> As if she were talking to herself, she began by saying that I was a woman, and that the women of Nkokolani are supposed to belong to someone in order to cease being

19 Ibid., 40.
20 Ibid., 28.
21 Ibid., 80.

> no one. That is why a single girl is termed *lamu*, which means 'she who hopes'. It's a way of saying that we shall be people only once we become wives. Don't lose hope, daughter. You haven't stopped being a *lamu* yet. The certainty of such condemnation was the best encouragement my mother could offer me.[22]

As seen here, Imani speaks of these traditions, which are passed on to her by her own mother, in a critical manner and even calls marriage a 'condemnation'. With marriage the woman loses all her individuality and becomes a vessel to perpetuate community (collectivity); she must also be obedient to the husband and act in submissive ways. In the words of Imani: 'I suddenly had a thought about the lifelong burden of responsibility. Rather than ask for love, the men of Nkokolani ask women to be punctual in serving their meals. In this, my father was the same as all the other man in Nkokolani. He existed in order to be served. He was passing along this time-honoured women's tradition to me.'[23]

Physical violence against women is also presented as being the norm within the VaChopi culture, and women in fact yearn to die to become spirit (dust, ash), a state when the body will no longer hurt. All Imani's female lineage was beaten and found ways of enduring pain or in fact committed suicide in order to stop being beaten, to escape the 'burden' of the body. The very name given initially to Imani by her mother was 'Ash', which was a way to protect her from the burden of inhabiting the female body:

> *Was your mother beaten?*
>
> *Your grandmother, great-grandmother and great-great grandmother. It's been like that ever since women were women. You'd better get ready to be beaten as well. [...] Chikaza Makwakwa interrupted my thoughts: Do you know how your grandmother died? She didn't wait for me to answer. She was struck by a flash of lightening, that's how she died.*
>
> *So why must you remember this now?*
>
> *Because that's how I want to die as well.*
>
> This is how she wanted her end to be: free of body, weightless, without a trace of her to bury. As if a painless death might erase all the pain in her life.

22 Ibid., 144.
23 Ibid., 220.

> Every time a storm broke, our mother would rush out into the fields and stand there, here arms spread, in imitation of a withered tree. She was waiting for the fatal thunderbolt. Ash, dust, soot: that is what she yearned to become. Her desired fate was to be reduced to an invisible powder, light, so light that she would travel the world, carried on the wind. It was my grandmother's wish that justified my name. That's what my mother wanted me to remember.
>
> *I like 'Ash',* I said, *I don't know why, but it reminds me of angels.*
>
> *I gave you that name to protect you, when we are dust, nothing can hurt us.*[24]

The VaNguni patriarchy is also attacked as it is in many ways similar to the VaChopi patriarchy with the physical and psychological abuse of women being quite the norm. The fact that the VaNguni rape and abduct VaChopi women is of course frequently discussed in the novel and also constitutes a critique of the way women are viewed by the VaNguni or what happens in times of war. Referring to African colonialisms and the mobility and transculturality of the African continent long before Arab and European colonisation, Achille Mbembe has argued the following in 'The Internet is Afropolitan':

> [W]hen you study the cultural history of the continent carefully, a number of things come to the fore in terms of how African societies have constituted themselves and how they operated. First, they constituted themselves through circulation and mobility. When you look at African myths of origin, migration occupies a central role in all of them. There is not one single ethnic group in Africa that can seriously claim to have never moved. Their histories are always histories of migration, meaning people going from one place to the other, and in the process amalgamating many other people. So circulation and amalgamation, you compile the gods, you conquer one ethnic group, you defeat them militarily, and you take their gods as yours, or you take their women as your wives, and therefore they become your parents.[25]

Mbembe's remarks can be directly applied to what is happening in *Woman of the Ashes*: as the VaNguni conquests progress, we witness various ethnic groups being incorporated into VaNguni and taking on their cultural behaviours.

24 Ibid., 13–14.

25 Achille Mbembe, 'The Internet is Afropolitan', *Chimurenga Chronicle* (17 March 2015), <http://chimurengachronic.co.za/the-internet-is-afropolitan/>.

Through the figure of Germano de Almeida, Portuguese patriarchy and masculinity are also critiqued, and especially the way African women are perceived. Germano arrives in Mozambique alone and is sent there as punishment for having been involved in the January 31st Republican Revolt in Porto in 1891. In some ways, he is a typical Portuguese man with set ideas about women, and especially African black women: seductive, overly sexual, irrational, and many other negative clichés. Germano finds Imani very attractive and seems to fall in love with her – or at least is very interested in having sexual relations with her. Imani functions in some ways as the exotic and sexualised African woman who should make herself available to the white man. Germano even comes to see Imani as a symbol for the African continent itself; both are portrayed as impossible to control or civilise, suggesting his own confusion and conflation between women and land. The aim of the colonisers was to possess both the woman and the land – a type of rape of both. As Germano notes in his letters to Counselor d'Almeida, Imani (and the African land) have entered his dreams, his unconscious in such a way that he feels he cannot escape them, yet he is unable to control either:

> And I was imprisoned in the hope that this false garrison might be mine, might be Portuguese, my home. But I was impotent. A far greater creature devoured the spider and its web. This creature's name is Africa. No wall, no fortress could stop it. And there it was, infiltrating through the cracks in the sounds of the marimbas and in the wailing of its children. There it turned into roots, which spread among the gaps in the bricks. There it was, dwelling in my dreams, invading my life in the shape of a woman.[26]

26 Couto, *Woman of the Ashes*, 169. Germano's impotence here may be related to the fact that within colonial, racist and Eurocentric discourse, Africa was thought of as a place of darkness, irrationality, femininity, a place closer to nature that should be brought to civilisation and order by the more advanced and ordered European man. Imani represents Africa and being closer to Imani then signals a loss of masculinity/manhood/rationality for Germano. It signals entrance into darkness and a regression to a more primal state, one of madness or degeneration, as we can see played out in Joseph Conrad's *Heart of Darkness* (London: Penguin Books, 1995), for instance. See also Valentin-Yves Mudimbe, *The Invention of Africa: Gnosis, Philosophy and the Order of Knowledge* (Bloomington: Indiana University Press, 1988).

Imani's father, Katini Nsambe, in fact tells her that she should do with Germano what is expected of a woman, implying that he had seen white men expecting to have easy access to black women and black men supposedly consenting. And he later directly tells her to go to Germano and offer herself: '*Now come here and drink, so you can forget who you are: a poor black woman smelling of the soil … Tomorrow go back to the Portuguese man's house and make that foreigner's head go giddy like the flames in fire.*'[27] This suggests of course the racial and gender hierarchies that come with European colonialism where white men are at the top, then white women, black men and at the bottom, black women.[28] The black man internalises this hierarchy and power dynamic and gives way to the white man, who is seen as the perfect, universal being, who has power, who is intelligent and fully civilised: the one to emulate. It can be argued that the coming of European patriarchy with all its racial and gender gradations exacerbates African patriarchies and even brings about a complex of inferiority, for as Fanon argued in *The Wretched of the Earth*[29] and *Black Skin, White Masks*,[30] those oppressed, having internalised a language of violence and domination, often also want to oppress those they see as less than themselves. Fanon sees this as our deep human tragedy, noting that violence only breeds violence, and colonialism, being violence par excellence, only understands the language of violence; traumatised by violence, the victim only understands violence and is unable to exit this vicious cycle, failing to envisage any other method of human interaction. This very idea is directly alluded to in the novel by an older VaChopi man when referring to the VaNdau, who had been conquered by the VaNguni and were now their soldiers: 'Those who had been enslaved by the VaNguni would be even crueler than their masters. Unfortunately, that is the way of the world: those who have suffered

27 Couto, *Woman of the Ashes*, 222.

28 For good discussions on this, see Anne McClintock, *Imperial Leather: Race, Gender, and Sexuality in the Colonial Context* (New York: Routledge, 1995), and my own article, 'Confused "Slaves" of Many Traditions: The Search for the Freedom Dance in Chiziane's *Niketche, A Tale of Polygamy*', *Research in African Literatures*, Vol. 41 no. 2 (2010), 133–159.

29 Frantz Fanon, *Black Skin, White Masks* (London: Paladin, 1970).

30 Frantz Fanon, *The Wretched of the Earth* (New York: Grove Press, 1968).

want others to suffer. We would be more harshly treated by the slaves of the VaNguni than by the VaNguni themselves. We would suffer so much at the hands of the blacks that we would forget how much we had suffered under the whites.'[31] It is important to consider here that the VaNguni are also dealing with Portuguese (and British) colonialisms and are also likely to have internalised racist ideologies about themselves brought about by the latter, which may make them more violent towards other Africans. This is in fact explored in Ungulani Ba Kha Khosa's novel, *Ualapai*, when Gungunhana, after being taken by the Portuguese and before his exile into the Azores where he will die in 1906, curses the blacks that were on the side of the Portuguese (such as the VaChopi), telling them how much worse off they will be under Portuguese rule, as evidenced in the following excerpt:

> Those men with the skin the colour of a young goat that you applaud today will enter your villages with the noise of their guns and a whip as long as the piton. They will call person by person, writing your names on a piece of paper making you crazy and imprisoning you. The names that come from your forgotten ancestors will forever die, because the men with the skin the colour of a young goat will give you the names that they please, calling you shit, and you will even thank them.[32]

The Portuguese also use VaChopi women and children to impose their rule or punish the VaChopi who are not paying their taxes on time. This is what happens to Imani's grandmother Layeluane, who is taken by the Portuguese for ransom during her husband Tsangatelo's[33] absence when he was serving in the Portuguese military:

> Tsangatelo had left to join the Portuguese military forces who were facing rebellion in the vicinity of Lourenço Marques. He thought he would be away for a month or two; he was away for nearly a year. The *indunas*, or officials from Inhambane turned up to collect the taxes. Layeluane was unable to pay and explained to the collectors the reasons for her husband's absence. They didn't believe her. They arrested and took

31 Couto, *Woman of the Ashes*, 156–157.

32 Ungulani, Ba Ka Khosa, *Ualalapi* (Lisbon: Editorial Caminho, 1987), 118 (my translation).

33 In the village where he lived by the sea, before moving to Nkokolani, Tsangatelo had a porterage business, transporting merchandise and slaves; he was what the Portuguese called *Pombeiro*.

> her away as a guarantee of payment. She was what the Portuguese termed 'taxes in arrears'. When the men were absent and families couldn't pay, the women and their children were taken away until their husbands turned up to pay their ransom.[34]

On a more positive note, the relationship between Imani and Germano is more complex and less dichotomous since both seem to have a genuine attraction towards one another, if only for the fact that they are 'others' to each other and as such are drawn to one another. For instance, Imani feels curious about Germano's hair and wants to run her fingers through it though he takes that as an invitation to physical intimacy, indicating perhaps his misguided expectations and ideas about black women. Yet, at the same time, Germano also comes to see Imani beyond basic racist and sexist stereotypes and finds her intelligent in many ways. Imani herself recognises that Germano is not the typical Portuguese or white man:

> I remember the day Sergeant Germano de Melo arrived at Nkokolani. In truth, it was immediately obvious that this Portuguese was different from all the other Europeans who had visited us. As he climbed out of his pirogue, he quickly rolled up his trousers and walked ashore. The other whites, whether Portuguese or English, would avail themselves of a black man's back to carry them to dry land. He was the only one who didn't bother with these services.[35]

The longer Germano stays in Mozambique, the more he comes to doubt the legitimacy of colonialism and the capacity of the Portuguese to civilise and effectively govern the Mozambican colony. As Imani notes, 'This white man, who had presented himself a matter of months ago with such an elegant bearing and such an impeccable uniform, sat there now, beaten and submissive, surrendering to the care of a black girl.'[36] We see here a partial inversion of the usual power dynamics, Imani seemingly holding more power than Germano.

In his correspondence with Counselor José d'Almeida, Germano also gives us a negative view of his father, a stern man, who represented an unhealthy type of masculinity, a man who did not want his mother to tell

34 Couto, *Woman of the Ashes*, 120.

35 Ibid., 40.

36 Ibid., 106–107.

him stories or show emotion towards him – a man who never laughed. Moreover, this type of masculinity displayed by Germano's father is often associated with despotic regimes, wars, empires, exaggerated national pride, and a conservative, fatalistic and overpowering Catholic ethic. This type of masculinity is depicted as being destructive and as inhibiting men's beingness (realisation as human beings):

> My father, stern and serious, wore black, as if we were mourning all the dead of this world. In the darkness of night, when the whole household slept, my mother would tiptoe to my room in order to say good night. Your father won't let me kiss you, she would murmur … In a hushed voice, she would tell me stories. They were simple fables, some to provoke laughter, others tears. By that time, I had already learned to hold back tears and swallow my laughter. I was born to live among shadows. My home had the smell and silence of an orphanage. I had everything I needed to be a good soldier.[37]

Imani is a victim of multiple oppressions, as are many of the black women in the novel. When explaining the story of her name, Imani says she does not really have a name: 'The name I was given isn't a name. In my mother tongue, Imani means "Who's there?" You knock on a door, and from inside someone asks: Imani? So my identity was merely a question. As if I were a shadow without a body, the endless wait for an answer.'[38] This implies that she lacks proper identity even within her own ethnic group: she is a being waiting to be. She then adds: 'I don't know why I am spending so much time explaining all this, for I wasn't born to be a person. I'm a race, I'm a tribe, I'm a sex, I'm everything that stops me from being myself. I'm a black woman, I belong to the VaChopi, a small tribe on the coast of Mozambique.'[39] These assertions illustrate that she sees herself as someone at the bottom of a multi-layered hierarchy reflecting various social constructs. She is aware that she has been made into a race by a Eurocentric racist paradigm which arrived with Portuguese colonialism; she is aware that she is seen mostly as a 'sex'/body by her own people, the VaChopi and by the Portuguese; and she is aware that she

37 Ibid., 89.

38 Ibid., 4.

39 Ibid., 5.

belongs to a small tribe that has much less power than the VaNguni or the Portuguese and is therefore at their mercy for survival. As she says, she 'was not born to be a person'. Her personhood and full humanity are arrested right at birth when she enters the multiple networks of power already operating, which prevent her from BEING. Entangled in the multiple intersectionalities of power dynamics which imprison her in their many merciless tentacles, Imani is a being waiting to be born, waiting to become. This brings to mind Simone de Beauvoir's now famous saying in *The Second Sex*, 'One is *not born*, but rather becomes, a *woman*',[40] except that in this case we are dealing with more than patriarchal oppressions (African and European) and have the added components of race, class and ethnicity. That Imani was born naked and beautiful (in other words, born equal in the sense of having right to attain full personhood, as Simone de Beauvoir might put it) does not matter, for she is brought close to nothingness at birth by patriarchal, racist, classist and ethnocentric constructs. I would also add that when Imani says she is a tribe, she is alluding to the fact that women in her ethnic group (as in others, especially in the context of independence battles or postcolonial narrations of identity) are often seen as bearers of culture (symbols of nation and cultural identity) and made to perform womanhood in a certain way to benefit a masculine idea of nation that continues to privilege men. Women are the token of nationhood, made to uphold traditions that may not be very beneficial to themselves for the sake of affirming cultural identity, an identity that is different (and wants to be seen as different) from that of the coloniser.[41] As discussed, Imani's awareness of the power dynamics restricting her freedom and her criticism of patriarchies (both local and foreign), are in themselves revealing of her agency and non-submission. Her reflective, intelligent and non-accommodating nature signals that she is a conscious being in search of herself, and as such, will find ways to assert agency however she can, unwilling just to accept things the way they are.

40 De Beauvoir, Simone, *The Second Sex*, ed and trans H. M. Parshley (London: Vintage, 1997).

41 It is important to note that even though women participated in Mozambique's wars of independence and were promised equality after independence, the postcolonial reality did not reflect such promises, and women's rights are still very much

I will now discuss some of the ways in which Imani shows resistance towards Portuguese/European colonialism. Aware of how the presence of the Portuguese (or Europeans) has shattered the world order of the VaChopi, implanting new ways of thinking and being, including a new language that carries values and visions from another world order, Imani often tries to assert the VaChopi way of life. Her very actions serve as an affirmation and reaffirmation of the pre-colonial way of life and function to contest the invading order. In her dealings with Germano de Melo, we see that she resists Portuguese culture even if on the surface she is an assimilated person who speaks Portuguese and went to Catholic mission school. For instance, she corrects Germano's pronunciation of Gungunhane's name, although she does not fully tell him what she thinks:

> I'm sorry. But the way to say his name is Ngungunyane, Sergeant, sir. If you can't say it, you can always call him Mudungazi. But it's important that we call our enemies by their correct names … Is that so? Well, then, listen: this gun is a Kropatschek. Now say 'Kropatschek', go on, see if you can … The difference was that I would never have to call a gun by its name, and Germano would have to utter the name of the African emperor every day. That's what I should have told him. But I held back submissively.[42]

disregarded. The nation of Mozambique was defined by a minority westernised elite, who disregarded both local Mozambican cultural realities and women's rights, in what Skjon Lee called 'the statement of nation' in 'The Vanguardist Imperative, Statement of Nation, and the Language Question' in Mozambique's *Sociedade Nova*, 1975–85, Paper presented at the Semiotics Workshops, University of Chicago, 10 January 2002. <http://cas.uchicago.edu/workshops/semiotics/E.%20Lee%20 Skjon%20Semiotics%20Paper%20on%20Mozambique-01-10-02.doc> (permission to quote and cite obtained from the author). For discussions on the links between national identity in pre-independence and postcolonial Mozambique and women's rights in Mozambique, see my article 'Confused "Slaves" of Many Traditions: The Search for the Freedom Dance in Chiziane's *Niketche, A Tale of Polygamy*', Vol. 41 no. 2 (2010), 133–159. For other links between women's rights and narratives of nationalism in postcolonial societies, see also Anne McClintock, '"No Longer in a Future Heaven": Gender, Race and Nationalism', in *Dangerous Liaisons: Gender, Nation, and Postcolonial Perspectives, ed. Anne McClintock, Aamir Mufti and Ella Shohat* (Minneapolis: University of Minnesota Press, 1997), 89–112.

42 Couto, *Woman of the Ashes*, 108.

In addition, Imani often explains to Germano her own culture, telling him fables and traditions of the land, and he frequently receives those explanations well, as if in a state of fascination with this different (and novel) way of seeing and being in the world, and admires the enthusiasm with which Imani explains them. Imani becomes a teacher to Germano and not the other way around. In the following passage we see how Imani tells Germano about the importance of the dead (the ancestors) for maintaining the order of the world, how they live in everything, nourishing the earth when falling as dew. She wants him to see the relational and holistic way that guides the VaChopi worldview:

> She told me that the dead don't walk on earth; it's they who make the earth walk. With a rope fashioned from sand and wind, the deceased fasten the sun so that it won't get lost in the heavens. She also said that the dead open up the way for the birds and the rains and they fall to the ground in every drop of dew, to fertilise the soil and give the bugs water to drink. The girl said all this without pausing for a breath. *Where did you learn all this*, I asked apprehensively? *I didn't have to learn*, she answered, *I am made of all of this. What I had to be taught were the white men's stories.*[43]

Another important way in which Imani shows resistance to cultural colonisation is seen in the way she contests the story of the Inharrime told by Bianca (an Italian woman staying in Mozambique), who claims that the river had been named River of Copper by Vasco da Gama. Bianca's account of the river's story and its naming by da Gama constitute an appropriation of a reality that does not belong to the Portuguese, the naming being a way to control (and colonise) a local reality. But the 'true story' of the river is quite different as Imani tells us in detail and quite beautifully:

> The Italian woman spoke of the names the river had. When she announced them, I felt uncomfortable. For she spoke as if the waters of the Inharrime belonged to her. The truth is, Bianca is far from knowing how these rivers are born. By endowing them with names, she neglected their history. The Italian woman doesn't know that in the beginning, when the earth as yet had no owners, the rivers and clouds flowed under the ground. Then the demon arrived and stuck its finger in the sand. His long nails scratched around in the depths. He was looking for stones that shimmered in the sunlight. Our mothers begged the gods to protect the stars they had hidden under the sand. They begged the devil to cease tearing out the minerals and delivering them

43 Ibid., 208–209.

> up to the covetousness of those seeking to enrich themselves. But the devil didn't stop there. For there were those among the power-hungry who worshipped him … The riches that lay underground were cursed. The clouds and rivers abandoned the planet's belly in order to escape this curse. And they became the earth's veins and hair. This is the story of the rivers. The greedy may steal their water until they dry. But they won't steal their history.[44]

There are many other things that the Italian woman does not understand about the VaChopi culture according to Imani. She does not understand, for instance, why Imani's father says that '[her] tears are not [hers]' but rather 'belong to a river flowing inside of [them] that overflows through the eyes'; she does not know that the river is a source and that 'source isn't a place we give a name to' but rather 'the original belly, where those who arrive and those who depart lie nestled'; she does not know many things about Nkokolani, things that 'cannot be explained in another language'.[45] Imani further tells us that she learned to write to 'better relate [what] she has lived', to 'tell the stories of those who have no form of writing', and to 'write the names of the dead so that they may be born again'.[46] Writing functions as a way to recreate/rescue the VaChopi cultural legacy threatened by colonial occupation, so that it may live on and also enter the realm of what Europeans considered history, given Hegel's claim in *The Philosophy of History* that only literate civilisations could enter the realm of history, Africa being 'no historical part of the World', without 'movement or development to exhibit'.[47] Imani also tells us about the marimba, the musical instrument her father plays, explaining in detail how it is made and the significance it has for the VaChopi, and through her narration we get to hear many other VaChopi people's abundant use of oral stories (fables) to explain the reality and culture of the VaChopi.

Tom Stennett correctly states the following:

> As the scribe who narrates the story of those who cannot write, Imani becomes a literal embodiment of Mozambican orature: of the names written in the earth by

44 Ibid., 253–254.

45 Ibid., 253.

46 Ibid., 254.

47 G. W. F. Hegel, *The Philosophy of History*, trans. J. Sibree, introduction C. J. Friedrich (New York: Dover Publications, 1956), 29.

> her father Katini and the oral narratives of her grandfather Tsangatelo (MC, 130–31; 141–42) that risk being forgotten because they have not been written down. Hilary Owen has argued that one of the challenges for Mozambican woman writers is the construction of a narrative subject 'at the intersection of written Portuguese and oral African vernaculars': 'the figure of "woman as writer" effectively finds itself reified as oral matrix in a way that militates against conscious female agency using linguistic hybridisation to women's own political ends'. In ventriloquising his fictional female scribe as the teller of the lost stories of Mozambique's history, Couto effectively makes Imani into the vehicle through which an oral matrix may be filtered. Thus, in Imani, Couto attempts to combine the traditionally masculine enterprise of narrating the Mozambican nation, through a critical revision of a key moment in Mozambique's history, with the oral sphere to which Mozambican women have often been relegated.[48]

However, Stennett then goes on to attack Mia Couto by noting:

> Feminine discourse [in *Mulheres de Cinza* and other of his novels] is still distilled through a male storyteller, a cis-man who takes a linguistically feminised name, Mia, and manoeuvres himself into a position as a writer who shares many of the traits of his own fictional women writers. As such, Imani's assertion that she writes for those who do not have access to the written word is a justification for Couto's own enterprise, as a writer of novels (such as *A Confissão da Leoa*) in which a fictional woman narrator exposes the brutal reality of a rural patriarchy. Imani is not an autonomous agent: she is a fiction created by Mia Couto. Thus, Imani's justification for writing on behalf of the pen-less is by extension Couto's too. I would argue that this boundary, the one between narrator and author, is one that Couto does not and cannot successfully dismantle – if nothing else because it is a frontier that lies outside the textual worlds he creates. It is one thing to create textual spaces in which one may dream of a world where gender is not a barrier, but it is another to suggest that the reader should forget the author's background in a world where gender clearly is important. Couto's stated aim is to give life to the silenced voices of orature through the written word.[49]

These arguments and attacks on the author seem out of place and unfair. Mia Couto is not claiming that his literary narrations (and his female narrators) are the same as the voice of real Mozambican black women or real Mozambican women writers such as Paulina Chiziane or Lília Momplé, as Stennett further notes, and Couto is not claiming he can substitute

48 Tom Stennett, 'Writing on Behalf of Those Women "Que Não [?] Têm Escrita": Gendered Boundaries Inside and Outside the Fiction of Mia Couto', *Portuguese Studies* 2, vol. 33, issue 1 (2017), 101–102.

49 Ibid., 103.

them either. He is a Mozambican white male writer who is aware of his privilege as such but is sensitive to the situation of Mozambican (black) women – a situation he explores in his novels in order to make us see how oppressive patriarchy is and how gender-based inequality greatly disfavours women; and in that process he paves the way for another way of being and of treating women. Literature does affect reality in some way and so questioning gender roles in fiction may well lead to change, or at least to a deep reflection about the issue that might generate change. Art does function as knowledge production: it affects how we see ourselves and others, it forms consciousness, and it constructs and deconstructs ideologies.

Imani also resists Portuguese dominance in more direct ways. Functioning as a spy, Imani often reads the correspondence between Germano de Melo and his superior Counselor José d'Almeida, and eventually finds out by reading a telegram that the Portuguese are not really interested in defending the VaChopi from the VaNguni, contrary to what Germano has been promising her and her people, and she relays this news to her family and other people in the community. As a form of punishment for Germano's lies, and in a calculated move, Imani pretends to be willing to be physically intimate with him and then suddenly withdraws, insulting him in her own language, a language that her assimilation into Portuguese culture had not been able to erase and would never erase:

> When the Portuguese saw me undressed and defenseless, he went mad. He hurriedly took off his clothes, his fingers shaking, his chin covered in drool. And as he held my waist, I let him lick my breasts until I felt my skin pulsating with his blood. Then the man lay down on the floor. He patted the ground, inviting me to lie down next to him. I declined. Instead, I looked down at him in drawn-out, queenly contemplation. In taking my time with carrying out his punishment, I felt the perverse thrill that a lioness feels before delivering the final blow. I tossed the telegram of the previous day onto the ground, placed a foot on his chest, spat in his face, and, in the gentlest voice, insulted him in my own language: *You lying white! You'll slither away like a snake* .... I had taken great delight addressing him in Txitxope. It was possible that no other black person had such a command of Portuguese. But the hatred I felt could be only expressed in my own language. I was doomed; I was destined to be born and to die in my own language.[50]

50 Couto, *Woman of the Ashes*, 140–141.

In what is the strongest act of direct resistance, Imani shoots Germano in the hand when he is about to fire into the crowd of VaChopi who are coming to the garrison to get firearms:

> Sergeant Germano de Melo looked in the direction of the square to confirm the greatest terror any European could feel: the sight of thousands of armed blacks emerging from the ground like dark ants, and advancing with the fury of a sudden storm.[51]
>
> *Keep away from here, both of you; go into the bedroom,* he ordered, with a voice that was unrecognisable. I ignored the order. I noticed how the Portuguese was aiming at the raucous, approaching throng with his weapon, already loaded and ready. And I saw that my brother Mwanatu was at the head of the crowd. I screamed: *Sergeant! Don't do it!* He didn't answer, but turned the barrel toward me, and his look betrayed his intention. He would fire at me if I distracted him from his fanatical objectives. From the wall, I took down the Martini-Henry, which had been hanging there the whole time. When I called his name again, the sergeant had already taken the first shot. He glanced at me out of the corner of his eye. Then his look turned to one of disbelief. He barely had time to shield his face with his hands, and when the gun went off, my body was thrown back and I was deafened by the explosion.[52]

Imani's own mother, Chikazi Makwakwa, also resists the violence of the VaNguni and avoids being raped by Gungunhane's soldiers by pretending to be pregnant and giving birth to a fish:

> *Don't hurt me, she begged. I'm pregnant. Pregnant? At your age?* They saw the little bump under her clothes, where she was hiding the fish she had been given. And, once again, they spat their doubt into her face: *Pregnant? You? How many months?...* Unnoticed by any of them, she grabbed the spiny dorsal fin of the fish and used it to tear her wrist. She waited for the blood to flow and then opened her legs, as if she were giving birth. Gradually, she pulled the fish from under her clothes, as if it were emerging from her insides. Then she lifted the fish up in her blood-soaked arms and announced: *Here is my child! My little boy is born*! The VaNguni soldiers stepped back in horror. This was no ordinary woman. She was a *noyi*, a witch. And there was no more sinister offspring she could have produced. A fish for these occupying soldiers was a taboo creature. And as if the animal weren't enough, its appearance was compounded at the same moment by the worst of all impurities: the blood of woman, the filth that soiled the universe.[53]

51 Ibid., 243.

52 Ibid., 244–245.

53 Ibid., 10–11.

Since Chikazi had grown in the South and was familiar with the VaNguni culture, she was likely aware that the fish was a taboo animal for the VaNguni and that they considered the blood of women as 'filth that soiled the universe', and so she uses all this to escape their violence.

Yet, the mother commits suicide later in the novel, disillusioned as she is with the many destructive effects of the war and her own displacement from the village by the coast which she continuously recalls and where she wants to return. She is also disenchanted with her husband, Katini, a musician who drinks too much and suffers from the emptiness and alienation caused by the cultural and racial oppression of the Portuguese and VaNguni colonialisms.

Woman of the Ashes reveals many of the ways in which women fight patriarchies, colonialism, national or ethnic identity and the intersections between these. If in *Woman of the Ashes* women are oppressed by both Mozambican/African and Portuguese/European ideologies related to gender, race and ethnicity, it is also true Imani and other women of the novel demonstrate, in many ways, that they are not mere passive and unconscious beings who believe and take in without question the ideologies that construct them as inferior others, who are at the bottom of highly racist, patriarchal and ethnocentric systems. From the 'woman of the ashes', the woman without voice, agency, story and history, they become beings inserted into history, beings reborn out of an almost nothingness created by different institutions of power, including the very disciplines of History and even Literature, which in many postcolonial nations have not duly acknowledged women's contributions in the fight against colonialism or in independence and liberation conflicts, focusing mostly on actions and accomplishments of men, and also offering limited views of what constitutes resistance. As noted in 'Women, Resistance and the Armed Struggle in Southern Africa' by Lyons Tanya and Mark Israel, Southern African women displayed many forms of colonial resistance and participated in armed struggles, even if often these roles were more of a supportive nature and less in direct combat:

> Women's participation was neither simply 'glorious' nor 'equal' with men. While some women did engage the enemy in military action, patriarchal attitudes structured the division of labour .... Women were far less likely than men to be involved in armed engagement and much more likely to be found in support roles and other

> uncelebrated but important tasks. They undertook these with little acknowledgment. Their work was carried out under the threat of violence from the minority regimes and sometimes in the face of sexist attitudes, sexual harassment and perhaps in some cases even sexual assault from their comrades .... We suggest that in wars of national liberation the content and context of resistance should be widened to include, at the very least, non-combat activities necessary to sustain military action. Any narrower view of resistance might either exclude the part played by many women in liberation or encourage the sort of glorification of relatively uncommon activities in which the Copenhagen paper engages.[54]

Works cited

Ba Ka Khosa, Ungulani. *Gungunhana*. Porto: Porto Editora, 2018.

Ba Ka Khosa, Ungulani. *Ualalapi*. Lisbon: Editorial Caminho, 1987.

Brugioni, Elena. 'O outro pé da sereia: história[s] na pós-colonialidade.' *Luso-Brazilian Review* 49, no. 1 (2012), 46–62. <https://muse.jhu.edu/issue/25977>.

Conrad, Joseph. *Heart of Darkness*. London: Penguin Books, 1995.

Couto, Mia. 'Mia Couto, Fnac Chiado, 20/10/2015. Apresentação do seu novo livro Mulheres de Cinza.' Out 10 2015. *You Tube*. <https://www.youtube.com/watch?v=gNqFz2aZnGQ>.

Couto, Mia. 'Mia Couto: *Mulheres de Cinza*.' *You Tube*. <https://www.youtube.com/watch?v=CCgOjEjLHsI>.

Couto, Mia. *Mulheres de Cinza*. Lisbon: Editorial Caminho, 2015.

Couto, Mia. *O outro pé da sereia*. Lisbon: Editorial Caminho, 2006.

Couto, Mia. *Woman of the Ashes*. Translated by David Brookshaw. New York: Farrar, Straus and Giroux, 2018.

De Beauvoir, Simone. *The Second Sex*. Edited and translated by H. M. Parshley. London: Vintage, 1997.

Fanon, Frantz. *Black Skin, White Masks*. London: Paladin, 1970.

Fanon, Frantz. *The Wretched of the Earth*. New York: Grove Press, 1968.

54 Tanya Lyons and Mark Israel, 'Women, Resistance and the Armed Struggle in Southern Africa', in *African Identities: Contemporary Political and Social Challenges (Making of Modern Africa)*, ed. Abebe Zegeye and Paul Ahluwalia (New York: Routledge, 2018), 48.

Hegel, G. W. F. *The Philosophy of History*. Translated by J. Sibree, introduction C. J. Friedrich. New York: Dover Publications, 1956.

Kaphagawani, N. Didier and Jeanette G. Malherbe. 'African Epistemology.' In *The African Philosophy Reader*, edited by P. H. Coetzee and A. P. J. Roux, 219–230. New York: Routledge, 2003.

Kombo, E. Ebitini. 'Women in National Liberation Wars in the Settler Colonies of Kenya and Zimbabwe: Pathways to Political Empowerment.' M.A. by Research, University of York, 2012. <http://etheses.whiterose.ac.uk/2600/1/Women_in_national_liberation_wars_Kenya_%26_Zimbabwe.pdf>.

Lyons, Lyons and Mark Israel. 'Women, Resistance and the Armed Struggle in Southern Africa.' In *African Identities: Contemporary Political and Social Challenges (Making of Modern Africa)*, edited by Abebe Zegeye and Paul Ahluwalia, 40–48. New York: Routledge, 2018.

Marques, Irene. 'Confused "Slaves" of Many Traditions: The Search for the Freedom Dance in Chiziane's *Niketche: A Tale of Polygamy*.' *Research in African Literatures* 41, no. 2 (2010). <https://www.jstor.org/stable/10.2979/ral.2010.41.2.133>.

Marques, Irene. 'Spaces of Magic: Couto's Relational Practices.' In *A Companion to Mia Couto*, edited by Grant Hamilton and David Huddart, 64–85. Suffolk: James Currey, 2016.

Marques, Irene. 'Suspending the "Lack" Through Art: African and Western Epistemological and Artistic Intersections (Mia Couto, Wole Soyinka, Léopold Senghor, Gaston Bachelard and Mark Epstein).' *African Studies* 27, issue 1. (2016): 127–142.

Marques, Irene. 'The Way/s of "Poetry": The Contracting and Expanding Self in the Writing of Mia Couto.' *Journal of the African Literature Association* 9, no. 2 (Summer/Fall, 2015): 75–111.

Marques, Irene. *Transcultural Discourses on Class, Gender, and Cultural Identity*. West Lafayette: Purdue University Press, 2011.

Mazrui A. Ali. 'Cultural Amnesia, Cultural Nostalgia and False Memory: Africa's Identity Crisis Revisited.' *African and Asian Studies* 12, issues 1–2, (2013): 13–19.

Mbembe, Achille. 'The Internet is Afropolitan.' *Chimurenga Chronicle* (17 March 2015). <http://chimurengachronic.co.za/the-internet-is-afropolitan/>

McClintock, Anne. '"No Longer in a Future Heaven": Gender, Race and Nationalism.' In *Dangerous Liaisons: Gender, Nation, and Postcolonial Perspectives*, ed. Anne McClintock, Aamir Mufti and Ella Shohat, 89–112. Minneapolis: University of Minnesota Press, 1997.

McClintock, Anne. *Imperial Leather: Race, Gender and Sexuality in the Colonial Contest*. New York: Routledge, 1995.

Mia Couto, interview by Scott Esposito, 'We Are Made of Memories: A Conversation with Mia Couto.' *The Paris Review*, May 2, 2013. <http://www.theparisreview.org/blog/20113/05/02/we-are-made-of-memories-a-conversation-with-mia-couto/>.

Mudimbe, Y. Valentin. *The Invention of Africa: Gnosis, Philosophy and the Order of Knowledge*. Bloomington: Indiana University Press, 1988.

Newitt, Malyn. *A History of Mozambique*. London: Hurst & Company, 1995.

Rothwell, Phillip. "Seaing into the Unconscious: The Role of Water in Mia Couto." In Phillip Rothwell, *A Postmodern Nationalist: Truth, Orality, and Gender in the Work of Mia Couto*, 91–132. Lewisburg: Bucknell University Press, 2004.

Skjon, Lee. 'The Vanguardist Imperative, Statement of Nation, and the Language Question' in Mozambique's *Sociedade Nova*, 1975–85. Paper presented at the Semiotics Workshops, University of Chicago, January 10, 2002. Permission to quote and cite obtained from the author, <http://cas.uchicago.edu/workshops/semiotics/E.%20Lee%20Skjon%20Semiotics%20Paper%20on%20Mozambique-01-10-02.doc>.

Stennett, Tom. 'Writing on Behalf of Those Women "Que Não [?] Têm Escrita": Gendered Boundaries Inside and Outside the Fiction of Mia Couto.' *Portuguese Studies* 2, vol. 33, issue 1 (2017), 85–104. <https://www.jstor.org/stable/10.5699/portstudies.33.1.0085>.

Teffo, J. Lebisa and Abraham P. J. Roux. 'Themes in African Metaphysics'. In *The African Philosophy Reader*, edited by P. H. Coetzee and A. P. J. Roux, 161–174. New York: Routledge, 2003.

The Battle of Algiers, directed by Gilles Montecorvo, 1966.

Turshen, Meredeth. 'Algerian Women in the Liberation Struggle and Civil War: From Active Participants to Active Victims?' *Social Research: An International Quarterly* 69, no. 3 (2002): 889–91. <https://muse.jhu.edu/>.

CELINA MARTINS

7 *Under the Frangipani* by Mia Couto: Myth and Poetics of Relation

Mia Couto's novel *A varanda do frangipani* [*Under the Frangipani*] (1996) celebrates the art of the storyteller in a rewriting of orality. The plot of the text is inscribed in the perspective of what has been generally called 'magical realism', through a poetics of appropriation, since it stages the dialogue between the *halakavuma* [my pet anteater] and the dead Ermelindo Mucanga.[1] As a symbol of the bond between man and the occult forces that conveys to the traditional tribal chief news about the future, the *halakavuma* proposes a second life to Ermelindo. Not having been buried according to traditional ceremonies, Ermelindo has become a ghost that wanders in unrest. The *halakavuma* advises the deceased to reincarnate in the body of the police inspector Izidine Naíta so as to put order in his existence. The inspector conducts an investigation into the death of the mulatto Vastsome Excellency, director of an old people's asylum, situated in a former colonial fort. The policeman interrogates all the elderly in turn, who confess their guilt, a fact which destabilises his task and transgresses the basics of detective fiction, since Izidine loses legitimacy to find the solution to his investigation. He is defeated by the autonomous voices of the elderly who interlace possible truths, standing as guardians of an oral culture threatened by the shocks of history: colonial war, civil war, and intensifying globalisation.

What draws attention in this novel is the presence of the frangipani, which is configured as a structuring *leitmotiv* that acts as a superior manifestation of life and influences the wandering of the characters. It is the principle around which the search for meaning gravitates: the leitmotiv of the tree leads us to sense that it is a mythical appropriation since myth is a

1 Mia Couto, *Under the Frangipani* (London: Serpent's Tail, 2008), 5.

narrative that provides a model that can solve contradictions. Myth offers a field of investigation that allows us to analyse several aspects of human culture, as Levi-Strauss observes:

> les mythes nous apprennent beaucoup sur les sociétés dont ils parviennent, ils aident à exposer les ressorts intimes de leur fonctionnement, éclairent la raison d'être de croyances, de coutumes et d'institutions dont l'agencement paraissait incompréhensible de prime abord.[2]
>
> [myths tell us a lot about the societies from which they originate, they help expose the intimate sources of their working, they shed light on the rationale for beliefs, customs and institutions whose form seemed incomprehensible at first glance (my translation)].

Following Edouard Glissant's thinking, our reading will show that the frangipani acquires a character status that enables relational fusion: 'le paysage cesse d'être un décor convenable et devient un personnage du *drama* de la Relation'[3] [the landscape ceases to be a suitable setting and becomes a character of the *drama* of Relation] (my translation). It will be thanks to the interaction between the subjects and their landscape that the narrative structure of the Poetics of Relation will develop: 'La Relation relie (relaie), relate'[4] [Relation links (relays), relates] (my translation). The Poetics of Relation is the principle of narration: each of Mia Couto's characters narrates short stories to Inspector Izidine, which circulate from narrator to narrator, multiplying in several versions of the same demand: the need to rescue oral culture. Each embedded story is told by different narrators in order to form a chain of relationships and to create a plural text made up of several contributions and various interpretations.

The frangipani is planted in a terrace, located inside the old St. Nicholas fort, in an undefined coastal zone which is never identified by a toponym. The tree occupies a strategic apical position, from which the protagonists' gaze can cover the sea and the savannah simultaneously. In its symbolism of opening horizons, the terrace is the place of sharing the spoken word,

2 Claude Lévi-Strauss, *L'Homme nu. Mythologiques IV* (Paris: Plon, 1971), 571.

3 Edouard Glissant, *Introduction à une Poétique du Divers* (Paris: Gallimard, 1996), 25.

4 Edouard Glissant, *La Poétique de la Relation* (Paris: Gallimard,1990), 187.

where dreams, rites, beliefs and mythical representations of the imaginary converge. It is the allegorical terrace that represents Mozambique,[5] as the appropriation of Eduardo Lourenço's phrase, pronounced in his farewell of Maputo, suggests: '*Moçambique: essa imensa varanda sobre o Índico*'[6] [Mozambique: this huge balcony overlooking the Indian Ocean].[7] Mia Couto retakes it as an epigraph of the fiction, indicating a metaphorical reading of infinite space.

The frangipani is planted in an old colonial fort, isolated from the rest of the country, since 'o lugar cortara relações com o universo'[8] [the place had severed its links with the world].[9] The fort was transformed into an asylum after independence, and the elderly have become exiled, 'islanded': the fort is surrounded on one side by minefields, remnants of the civil war, and on the other by the Indian Ocean. It is impossible to reach the fort by land and no boat can anchor because of the imposing rocks. The only possible access is by air: 'De helicóptero iam chegando mantimentos e visitantes'[10] [All supplies and visitors arrived by helicopter].[11]

The frangipani is the scene of several ruptures. It is the voice of the dead Ermelindo Mucanga that inaugurates the chronotope setting when suggesting that to cross its space is to delve into the overlapping of various pasts:

> A árvore do frangipani ocupa uma varanda de uma fortaleza colonial. Aquela varanda já assistiu a muita história. Por aquele terraço escoaram escravos, marfins e panos. Naquela pedra deflagaram canhões lusitanos sobre navios holandeses. Nos fins do tempo colonial, se entendeu construir uma prisão para encerrar os revolucionários que combatiam contra os portugueses. Depois da Independência ali se improvisou um asilo para velhos. Com os terceiros-idosos, o lugar definhou. Veio a guerra, abrindo pastos para mortes. Mas os tiros ficaram longe do forte. Terminada a guerra, o asilo restava como herança de ninguém. Ali se descoloriam os tempos, tudo engomado a silêncios e ausências.[12]

5 Alzira Seixo, *Outros erros. Ensaios e literatura* (Lisbon: Edições Asa, 2001), 358.
6 Mia Couto, *A varanda do frangipani* (Lisbon: Caminho, 1996), 9.
7 Couto, *Under the Frangipani, vide* epigraph.
8 Couto, *A varanda do frangipani*, 22.
9 Couto, *Under the Frangipani*, 14.
10 Couto, *A varanda do frangipani*, 22.
11 Couto, *Under the Frangipani*, 14.
12 Couto, *A varanda do frangipani*, 13.

[The frangipani occupies the terrace of a colonial fort. This terrace has witnessed much history. Slaves, ivory and cloth were all shipped out through it. From its stonework, Portuguese cannons blazed against Dutch ships. Towards the end of colonial times, it was decided to build a prison there to shut away the revolutionaries who were fighting against the Portuguese. After Independence, it was turned into a makeshift refuge for elderly people. With their arrival, the place went into decline. Then civil war came, producing a harvest of death. But the fighting took place far from the fort. When the war ended, the refuge remained, unclaimed by anyone as an inheritance. Here, time was drained of its colour, everything starched by silence and emptiness.][13]

The frangipani becomes the sacred place of the celebration of rhizome identity. For Glissant, the hypothesis of overcoming colonial logic is to shake hegemonic thinking by accepting creolisation as an unavoidable phenomenon that can only be fruitful if the unpredictable presence of heterogeneous cultural elements is valued in a parity perspective that prevents the degradation or the inferiorisation of being.[14]

Glissant distinguishes the metaphor of the single root and the rhizome root, reworked from the proposal of Deleuze and Guattari.[15] These scholars oppose arborescent systems, privileged by Chomsky's linguistics and by biology, by determining a higher centre, a hierarchy and an order of signification. They defend, instead, the rhizome metaphor that spreads in multiple networks.[16] In an appropriation game, Glissant recreates the notion of rhizome as image of plural identity at a time when the impurity of cultures ceases to be a stigma and becomes unavoidable and desirable.

According to Glissant, the root-identity proclaims the right to own land and legitimises the conquest of territory: '*L'identité racine*: – est préservée, par la projection sur d'autres territoires qu'il devient légitime de conquérir et par le projet d'un savoir[17] [The root-identity: – is preserved by the projection on to other territories that become legitimate to conquer and by the project of knowledge] (my translation). While the root-identity

13 Couto, *Under the Frangipani*, 3.

14 Glissant, *Introduction à une Poétique du Divers*, 18–19.

15 Gilles Deleuze and Félix Guattari, *Capitalisme et schizophrénie. Mille plateaux* (Paris: Minuit, 1980), 25.

16 Ibid., 25.

17 Glissant, *La Poétique de la Relation*, 157–158.

establishes a relationship of violence with the Other by denying his/her existence and preserving the purity of the race, thus becoming a single root that kills, the rhizome identity is represented as an underground and aerial root that branches in several senses that retains the idea of rooting but 'refuse l'idée d'une racine totalitaire'[18] [refuses the idea of a totalitarian root] (my translation). The rhizome spreads and contacts other roots without killing them. The rhizome hatches the Poetics of Relation by proposing 'toute identité (qui) s'étend dans un rapport à l'autre'[19] [any identity (that) extends in a relation with the Other] (my translation). The rhizome identity is an identity in becoming, based on the opening to the Other, accepting him/her in his/her difference: it is the identity "qui naît dans un lieu où l'on donne avec"[20] [that springs from a place where one gives with] (my translation). The rhizome is inscribed in the thought of Diversity that embraces the multiple and rejects universalising dogmas and thoughts by accepting all the imaginary worlds of the universe. For Couto, who is a biologist by training and therefore has a very concrete understanding of how this process deploys itself, 'o rizoma irmaniza […] o rizoma é abraço'[21] [the rhizome is brotherhood […] the rhizome is embrace (my translation)].

It will be from the perspective of fraternity and plural relation that the frangipani will build a fruitful space of openness, despite the connotation of exile that gushes from the description of the asylum. The interpenetration between the plant world and the protagonists gives rise to six types of relationship with the earth: the 'Mozambicanised Portuguese man' (Domingos Mourão); the mulatto tormented by purity of colour (Vastsome Excellency, director of the asylum), defender of a racist negritude; the *assimilado* withdrawn from popular culture by influence of studies carried out in Europe (the black inspector, Izidine Naíta);[22] the *assimilada* who becomes resistant

18 Ibid., 23.

19 Ibid., 23.

20 Ibid., 23

21 Preface to Celina Martins, *O entrelaçar das vozes mestiças. Análise das poéticas da alteridade na ficção de Edouard Glissant e Mia Couto* (Estoril: Principia, 2006), 7.

22 To integrate with the Portuguese colonial system, the black people, *assimilados*, had to renounce their religion, mother tongue and cultural roots.

(the nurse, Marta); the elderly who embody the richness of cultural heritage but wander on the margins of the world (the old-child Navaia, Gaffer and the sorceress Little Miss No); and the lost soul of Ermelindo Mucanga who cannot rest quietly in his tomb.

The Portuguese man Domingos Mourão is able to synthesise visions of his space of origin and participate in the Mozambican worldview by protecting the frangipani. As he admires its changes, evoking the passing of time in a metaphorical way, since the tree is the only plant that sheds its foliage, Domingos projects upon it his yearning, as he recalls the autumn of the Portuguese temperate climate. Thus, the space of the tree builds an imaginary bridge between Africa and Europe that mitigates the burden of his exile.

> [...] o Moçambique que amei está morrendo. Nunca mais voltará. Resta-me só este espaçozito em que me sombreio de mar. Minha nação é uma varanda.
>
> Nesta pequena pátria me venho espraiando todos estes anos, feito um estuário: vou fluindo, ensonado, meandrando sem atrito.
>
> Na sombra, me reinquintei, encostado àquele murmurinho como se fosse embalo de nascença.[23]
>
> [[...] the Mozambique I loved is dying. It'll never come back. All that's left is this little patch of ground where I seek the shade of the sea. My nation is this terrace here, this balcony over the ocean.
>
> All these years, I've spread out across this tiny fatherland like an estuary: I'm flowing, sleepy, at odds with nothing as I meander along.
>
> Here in this shade, I created my own kingdom, enraptured by that gentle murmur, as if it were a lullaby sung at my birth.][24]

The insistence on the semantic field of water, which implies various liquid windings, confirms our initial suggestion: the terrace makes it possible to transcend the enclosure since it is the opening for a symbolic birth. Domingos projects into the landscape his desire of transmigration of the soul: he imagines himself as a river embracing the ocean.

23 Couto, *A varanda do frangipani*, 50.
24 Couto, *Under the Frangipani*, 44.

It is through a story that Domingos explains his metamorphosis into a tree:

> Me contaram, é coisa antiga, dos tempos de Vasco da Gama. Dizem que havia, nesse tempo, um velho preto que andava pelas praias a apanhar destroços de navios. Recolhia restos de naufrágios e os enterrava. Acontece que uma dessas tábuas que ele espetou no chão ganhou raízes e reviveu em árvore.
>
> Pois, senhor inspector, eu sou essa árvore. Venho de uma tábua de outro mundo mas o meu chão é este, minhas raízes renasceram aqui. São estes pretos que todos os dias me semeiam.[25]
>
> [Let me tell you a story. It's from the old days, from the time of Vasco da Gama, so I was told. They say that in those days there was an old black man who wandered along the beaches picking up flotsam and jetsam. He collected the remains of shipwrecks and buried them. It so happened that one of the wooden planks he stuck in the ground grew roots and came back to life as a tree.
>
> Well, now mister inspector, I'm that tree. I come from a plank in another world but my ground is here, my roots were reborn in this place. It's these black men here who scatter my seeds every day.][26]

As an apprentice storyteller, Domingos reunites the Portuguese and Mozambican imaginary worlds, for he goes back to the golden age of discovery and narrates his regeneration in the form of a plant which took place with the help of black men. As a consequence, he presents himself as a rhizome-identity, a harmonious synthesis of two worlds that feed on each other.

Domingos' account gains new significant nuances if one associates it with the choice of his family name. The surname of the Portuguese character is 'Mourão', that is to say, it refers to the stake that delimits lands and, therefore, to the 'board' of the embedded story. The full integration of this Portuguese character into the African worldview implies a baptism: the elderly give him the new name Sidimingo, an affectionate diminutive of Domingos in the Changana language. In this way, like the black people in his embedded story, the asylum dwellers 'sow' him in oral culture.

25 Couto, *A varanda do frangipani*, 48.
26 Couto, *Under the Frangipani*, 42.

The involvement with nature frees Domingos' sensitivity, which leads him to develop a whole flow of images around the frangipani as an integrating work of art. As he breathes in the invigorating scent of the tree in a ritual gesture repeated by the other asylum companions, he delights in contemplating the beauty of the flowers that inspire him with the drive of a new life: 'Não era só o mar que me trazia esse desejo de me infindar. Eram as flores do frangipani. Como se me tivesse parenteado com a terra. Como se quem florescesse fosse eu mesmo'[27] [It wasn't just the sea that brought about my desire for infinity. It was the frangipani flowers. As if I had become one of the earth's family. As if I were the one in flower].[28]

Domingos wants to project himself into a vegetal imaginary world so as to transcend old age and exile by means of his fusion with the matrix of the frangipani. His soul flourishes, enabling him to take root: 'Bien fleurir est [...] une sûre manière de s'enraciner', said Gaston Bachelard[29] [To flourish well is [...] a sure manner to take root (my translation)]. When he touches the tree trunk, Domingos experiences transmutation thanks to the flight of his imagination. He becomes a creative force 'como se a partir daquela singular árvore ele fabricasse uma floresta inteira, sombras e chilreinos'[30] [as if he wished to create a whole forest, a kingdom full of shadows and twittering birds from that one single tree].[31]

A model of ascensional creation, the frangipani propitiates and intensifies the protagonist's poetic reverie which transfigures the universe from a stance of wonder: 'As flores do frangipani eram alimento para os olhos do português: ele as via cair, como escamas do sol, brancas transpirações das nuvens'[32] [The frangipani flowers were food for the old Portuguese fellow's eyes: he watched them fall like scales from the sun, white pearls of sweat from the clouds].[33] The novel establishes the *topos* of man's intimate communion with the landscape: Domingos overcomes the marginalised

27 Couto, *A varanda do frangipani*, 52.
28 Couto, *Under the Frangipani*, 46.
29 Gaston Bachelard, *La Terre et les rêveries du repos* (Paris: José Corti, 1948), 291.
30 Couto, *A varanda do frangipani*, 66.
31 Couto, *Under the Frangipani*, 60.
32 Couto, *A varanda do frangipani*, 65.
33 Couto, *Under the Frangipani*, 59–60.

experience of the asylum because he creates ties rooted in the dynamics of nature. Imagining himself as the frangipani, he extends his arms-branches towards the sea and sky, deepening his roots in the African cultural soil.

The tree also favours the tightening of cultures. At first, it brings about a brief confrontation between the black fellow Gaffer and Domingos, an argument that soon gains the contours of deep complicity. After having challenged colonial prejudices, they both initiate a dialogue that allows the exchange of myths. Despite having tried mistreating the frangipani, Gaffer makes clear that Africans venerate trees 'como se fossem família'[34] [like members of the family][35] and shares with him his personal version of *Genesis* grounded in a myth that displays how a still structured culture celebrates the essential unity between man and the cosmos:

> Primeiro, o mundo era feito só de homens. Não havia árvores, nem animais, nem pedras. Só existiam homens. Contudo, nasciam tantos seres humanos que os deuses viram que eram de mais e demasiado iguais. Então, decidiram transformar alguns homens em plantas, outros em bichos. E ainda outros em pedras. Resultado? Somos irmãos, árvores e bichos, bichos e homens, homens e pedras. Somos todos parentes saídos da mesma matéria.[36]

> [In the beginning, the world only contained men. There were no trees, no animals, no stones. Men alone existed. But so many humans were born that the gods realised there were too many and they were all the same. So they decided to turn some men into plants, others into animals. And some, even, in stones. The result? We're all brothers, trees and animals, animals and men, men and stones. We're all related, created out of the same matter.][37]

In reciting this vision of brotherhood, Gaffer foreshadows the harmonious outcome of the novel through the effect of *mise en abyme*.

In opposition to this conception of interdependence, the mulatto Vastsome Excellency intends to instigate enmity in the asylum by forcing Gaffer to take down the frangipani. He thus plans to cut the ties that bind old Domingos to the tree, perpetuating a revenge against the

34 Couto, *A varanda do frangipani*, 69.
35 Couto, *Under the Frangipani*, 63.
36 Couto, *A varanda do frangipani*, 69.
37 Couto, *Under the Frangipani*, 63–64.

Portuguese fellow because he still considers him a representative of colonialism. The administrator embodies a living paradox that is not resolved by synthesis: albeit a mestizo, he ideologically praises racial purity. But that purity is merely the radical negation of the white. Vastsome blindly promotes a root-identity, adopting the colonial ideology under the sign of ethnic confrontation. He is, in fact, a son of the impoverished land because he has lost all contact with the culture of the country, metaphorised in the frangipani. On the contrary, he encourages its destruction by engaging in arms trafficking, encouraging new armed conflicts. He lives divided because 'fora ensinado a dar-se mal com sua própria pele'[38] [had been taught to be ill at ease within his own skin][39] and he mistreated the Portuguese fellow so he would not be accused of privileging the whites. Presented by the asylum dwellers as an alienated subject and undermined by hatred, it is no wonder that he is the only one who tragically dies murdered by his accomplices, the corrupt men of the city.

It will be two women, Marta and Little Miss No, two strongly rooted plants, who will take on the role of mediators, because they will build bridges amongst the other asylum dwellers, confusing the inspector's wandering around in a labyrinthine search for the elucidation of the crime committed against Vastsome and guiding him towards the redemption of traditional culture.

Having overcome the temptation of self-destruction in which she had precipitated herself, Marta freely exiles herself in the fort as she could not bear the evils of discord and corruption that devastated her homeland. She revitalises herself by entering the cycle of dreams by the hands of the elders. She becomes, therefore, a lucid *assimilada* who raises awareness in Izidine when she reflects on the disruption caused by the war: the fragile thread that maintained communication between the people and the elderly, the last guardians of the inheritance of the past, had been torn. Marta's link with the Mozambican worldview emerges in a symbolic episode, in which the flowers of the frangipani appear in a dream as an offering of the elderly.

38 Couto, *A varanda do frangipani*, 131.
39 Couto, *Under the Frangipani*, 128.

When she wakes up, the nurse learns of her son's death and the same white petals remain next to her, comforting, a sign of an unbreakable solidarity between her and the asylum dwellers.

Since the loss of her son, Marta perpetuates the tradition of the mourning women of her village by sleeping naked outside in the open in communion with the energy of the ground. As soul mate, she welcomes the cradling of Mother-Earth and is reborn purified, reflecting the positive and universal symbolism of the fecundity of the earthly depths.[40]

Insistently, Marta sends to the sceptical Izidine clues of another reality he is unaware of, as he is remote and lost in Maputo's microcosm. She diverts his attention from the criminal investigation and paves the way for his transformation thanks to the knowledge of the sorceress Little Miss No.

In the process of the inspector's gradual metamorphosis, it is up to the old woman to reveal the corruption of his colleagues in Maputo, saving him from a death foretold by the *halakavuma*, an emissary of the ancestral spirits. Despite his rationalist view, in a parodic perspective[41] Izidine comes into contact with oral logic by going through initiation trials conducted by the asylum dwellers: he dies symbolically in order to be reborn as another and to be able to weave deeper threads with the Mozambican worldview. In that sense, his amorous liaison with Marta is a metaphor for the binding and deepening of two roots, torn from his native culture by the assimilation system.

It is important to underline that Little Miss No knows the secrets of plants and uses her knowledge to overcome obstacles. When Vastsome forces a fight between Domingos and Gaffer, the storm prevents disharmony. The healer gives each of the elders the *Kwangula tilo* [*kwangula* leaves],[42] which protect them from having their lungs burst, because, according to ancient belief, this plant is associated with thunder.

The dimension of the marvellous is entwined with rational logic, leaving the outcome of the novel open: if we adopt the mythical-magical

40 Gilbert Durand, *Les stuctures anthropologiques de l'imaginaire* (Paris: Dunod, 1969), 261.

41 See Phillip Rothwell, *Leituras de Mia Couto. Aspetos de um pós-modernismo moçambicano* (Coimbra: Almedina, 2015), 41.

42 Couto, *Under the Frangipani*, 84.

positioning of the elders, the frangipani is devastated by the storm lightning which outlines the contours of the *wamulambo*, the snake of heavenly storms. If we consider the rational perspective, the tree was struck by the explosion of the helicopter that was carrying Izidine's killers. The text does not provide a single interpretive key. The important thing is to emphasise that disorder has destroyed the tree: 'um testemunho que a morte visitara aquele lugar'[43] [a witness to the destruction visited upon that place.][44]

If, initially, Ermelindo appears as a cursed spirit for not having benefited from the funeral ceremony of the Mucanga tribe, his interaction with the sacred animal, the *halakavuma*, will allow him to reach long-awaited serenity because it has invited him to inhabit Izidine's body. Regarding the disappearance of the sacred tree, Ermelindo's spirit (re)establishes an alliance with his culture by recalling the teachings of the *halakavuma*: 'A árvore era o lugar de milagre'[45] [The tree was a place of miracles].[46] And, suddenly, a carnal relationship is established between Ermelindo and the blossoming of the tree: 'Então, desci do meu corpo, toquei a cinza e ela se converteu em pétala. Remexi a réstia do tronco e a seiva refluiu, como sémen da terra. A cada gesto meu o frangipani renascia'[47] [So I got down from my body, and touched the ashes, turning them into petals. I turned over the remains of the trunk, and the sap, like the earth's semen, began to flow once more. With every gesture I made, the frangipani became reborn].[48]

Ermelindo's journey to the world of the living turns out to be fruitful for two reasons: he regains his cultural identity, shattered by colonial rupture, and he enters into communion with the frangipani. At that moment of magical regeneration, the tree rises 'natalícia'[49] [newly born into the fullness of life].[50] Ermelindo, on the other hand, covers himself with the same ashes in order to favour his transformation into plant. It propitiates

43 Couto, *A varanda do frangipani*, 150.
44 Couto, *Under the Frangipani*, 149.
45 Couto, *A varanda do frangipani*, 151.
46 Couto, *Under the Frangipani*, 149.
47 Couto, *A varanda do frangipani*, 151.
48 Couto, *Under the Frangipani*, 149.
49 Couto, *A varanda do frangipani*, 151.
50 Couto, *Under the Frangipani*, 149.

the timelessness of the eternal return, for he returns renewed to the realm of the dead and he revives in the frangipani which welcomes, in its bosom, the aged bodies of Domingos, Gaffer, Navaia and Little Miss No, and thus becomes the bountiful cradle and tomb of various beings united by the blessing of the earth. The frangipani remains, setting the last utopian dream of brotherhood between diverse cultures as plaited rhizomes.

The quest of the old asylum dwellers (Domingos, Little Miss No, Navaia and Gaffer) and of the ghost Ermelindo is characterised by interiorisation and progressive metaphorisation: they become rhizome-identities after having shared an intense and fruitful reciprocal bond with the tree. All contact with the frangipani acquires a positive resonance because it indicates a search for rooting: the characters germinate as new seeds, and become shoots that feed on the interpenetration between cultures. In the novel, Mia Couto represents a marginal but tight community which resists domination because it still articulates its worldview through deeply rooted beliefs and traditions, constituting: 'un arrière-pays culturel ancestral' [an ancestral cultural hinterland (my translation)]. In transcending the effects of the colonial and civil wars, Couto restores a relationship of solidarity with the sacred, represented by the frangipani.

Couto's fiction thus outlines a poetics of Relation: if the present world derives from the overlap and intersection of heterogeneous cultural traits that influence each other, the quest for Mozambicanity will only make sense if it recognises as a basis cultural *métissage* between the imaginary worlds of Africa, Europe and Asia that configure the image of Mozambique, young and plural, still as a project of constructing identity. Likewise, cultures that have settled their dominion through imperialist expansion can only abandon their ethnocentric position if they accept cultural *métissage* as a structuring element of their identity.

At the end of the novel, Couto allegorises Mozambique as an open island, capable of being reborn from the ashes in the manner of the frangipani, a homeland that affirms itself a possible space of brotherhood between diverse cultures and worldviews:

> E hoje temos em Moçambique um mosaico de raças, etnias e culturas que estão em situação de namoro e viagem. No final desse noivado estaremos todos mudados [...]

Nenhuma etnia, nenhuma raça está, à partida, mais preparada para empreender esta viagem. Nenhuma etnia, nenhuma raça detém, à partida, o passaporte que confere o automático ingresso na moçambicanidade. [...] A Europa e a Ásia existem dentro de nós, africanos, como fios de um tecido em construção. [...] a aprendizagem será esta: aceitarmos todas as Áfricas, todas as Europas, todas as Ásias que existem em nós. E não olhar nunca essas heranças históricas como qualquer coisa que devemos erradicar, como mancha que devemos depurar em nome da pureza inicial. Do mesmo modo, a Europa necessita de aceitar as Áfricas (e Ásias) que habitam a sua actualidade. Todos os continentes necessitam, afinal, de assumir a sua mestiçagem racial, cultural e religiosa. [...] A revelação e entrecruzamento de valores e tradições requer uma relação entre seres soberanos. Uma relação que aceite o intercâmbio, namoro e hibridação de culturas. Esse intercâmbio não implicará a perda de identidade de nenhuma das partes.[51]

[And today in Mozambique there is a mosaic of races, ethnic groups and cultures that are in a situation of wooing and journeying. When this wooing comes to an end, we will all be changed [...]. No ethnic group or race is indeed better prepared to undertake such journey. No ethnic group or race truly holds the passport that grants automatic access to Mozambicanity. [...] Europe and Asia both exist within us, Africans, as threads of a fabric being woven. [...] what we will learn will thus be: to accept all Africas, all Europes, and all Asias that exist within us. And never perceive such historical heritages as something to be eradicated, as a stain that we must cleanse in the name of original purity. Likewise, Europe needs to accept the Africas (and Asias) that inhabit its present. In truth, all continents need to assume their racial, cultural and religious *métissage* [...] The revelation and intertwining of values and traditions require a relationship between sovereign human beings. A relationship that accepts the interchange, wooing and hybridisation of cultures. Such interchange will not imply any loss of identity of any of the parties] (My translation).

Works cited

Angius, Fernanda and Matteo Angius. *O desanoitecer da palavra*. Praia-Mindelo: Portugal Embassy, Portuguese Cultural Centre, 1998.

Bachelard, Gaston. *La Terre et les rêveries du repos*. Paris: José Corti, 1948.

51 Fernanda Angius and Matteo Angius, *O desanoitecer da palavra* (Praia-Mindelo: Portugal Embassy, Portuguese Cultural Centre,1998), 111.

Couto, Mia. *A varanda do frangipani*. Lisbon: Caminho, 1996.

Couto, Mia. *Under the Frangipani*. Translated by David Brookshaw. London: Serpent's Tail, 2008.

Durand, Gilbert. *Les structures anthropologiques de l'imaginaire*. Paris: Dunod, 1969.

Glissant, Edouard. *La Poétique de la Relation*. Paris: Gallimard, 1990.

Glissant, Edouard. *Introduction à une Poétique du Divers*. Paris: Gallimard, 1996.

Glissant, Edouard. *Le Discours antillais*. Paris: Gallimard, 1997.

Lévi-Strauss, Claude. *L'Homme nu. Mythologiques IV*. Paris: Plon, 1971.

Martins, Celina. *O entrelaçar das vozes mestiças. Análise das poéticas da alteridade na ficção de Edouard Glissant e Mia Couto*. Estoril: Principia, 2006.

Rothwell, Phillip. *Leituras de Mia Couto. Aspetos de um Pós-modernismo Moçambicano*. Translated and introduced by Margarida Calafate Ribeiro. Coimbra: Almedina, 2015.

Seixo, Alzira. *Outros erros. Ensaios e literatura*. Lisbon: Edições Asa, 2001.

FERNANDA VILAR

8 The Ghosts of Ngungunyane: Constructing an Ambivalent Hero[1]

> 'A sua memória viverá nos sonhos dos que não têm escrita.
> E viverá nos livros dos que perderam os sonhos.'[2]
> ['Its memory will live in the dreams of those who have no writing.
> And it will live in the books of those who have lost their dreams'].

When countries construct their heroes, they are generally drawn to unanimously admired and coherent figures. The anti-colonialist people fighting for power in Mozambique began to revive the memory of Ngungunyane as an inspirational figure during the liberation struggle. Afterwards, FRELIMO (the Liberation Front of Mozambique) came to consider him a national hero, and a guide in the civil war that followed the country's independence. Ngungunyane was chosen as a figure of national unification and functioned as a 'symbol of love' for Mozambique. At the request of Samora Machel, Mozambique's first post-independence president, a handful of sand from the Azores cemetery was taken to Maputo in 1985 to celebrate the tenth anniversary of Mozambican independence. This sand symbolised Ngungunyane's remains: he died on the Azorean island of Terceira in 1906. Coincidentally, several political figures in Mozambique hail from the Gaza province where Emperor Ngungunyane

1 This article was prepared partially for project MEMOIRS – Children of Empires and European Postmemories, funded by the European Research Council (ERC) under the European Union's Horizon 2020 research and innovation programme (grant agreement No 648624).

2 Priest Rudolfo Fernandes in Mia Couto's *As Areias do Imperador: uma trilogia moçambicana. livro dois, A Espada e a Azagaia* (Alfragide, Portugal: Caminho, 2016), 283.

reigned: not only Machel but also Eduardo Mondlane, co-founder and first president of FRELIMO, and Joaquim Chissano, the second president of Mozambique.

Ngungunyane, the Emperor of Gaza, took power a few months before the Berlin conference (1884–1885), when European states divided portions of Africa among themselves. Threatened by British and German interest in the region, the Portuguese rapidly had to create a strategy to show their dominance over Mozambican territories. Ngungunyane became their principal enemy. Understanding the conflict of interests between Europeans, the Emperor sought to take advantage of the situation with diplomatic missions to Britain and Portugal. The Portuguese offensive occurred only ten years later in early 1895 – just at the moment when the Emperor lost the loyalty of his subjects and violent conflicts established themselves in his kingdom. Although he had spent years resisting foreign invasion, he was eventually captured and deported. He died in exile, but not before he was shown in a cage at the Belem botanical garden in Lisbon.

Over a century after the Portuguese defeated and imprisoned the Emperor, the Mozambican people still remembers the oppression and violence that characterised his reign and affected the life of his subjects. This memory was clear during the inauguration of his bust in Mandlakazi, Gaza province, in 1995, celebrating the 100th anniversary of the resistance put up by the Gaza empire.[3] This commemoration was the then-president Joaquim Chissano's idea. It was badly received, and locals disfigured the statue. Their gesture rejected Chissano's attempt to continue to impose as national hero a figure whose memory was highly ambivalent. The political dimension of deconstructing the myths associated with Ngungunyane is also a critique of FRELIMO's unitary (and authoritarian) vision of Mozambique. If for some people Ngungunyane represents resistance to colonialism, for others he is associated with internal wars and destruction.

Young African states have followed different historical paths but demonstrate clear parallels. Each seeks to update and rewrite the multiple histories, which remain alive in the present. The colonial past, far from being

3 Several important Mozambican figures come from the Gaza province: Eduardo Mondlane, co-founder and first president of FRELIMO, Samora Machel and Joaquim Chissano, first and second presidents of Mozambique.

a past or dead experience, generates ghosts that we might understand as the products of an imperial legacy in these recently-constructed nations. In appealing to a figure as controversial as Ngungunyane, Mozambicans chose to narrate and reinvent the nation through an earlier symbol of resistance to colonialism. However, they have not been able to expunge all 'impurities' from his history because his deeds live on in the discourses that have been handed down by their contemporaries.

This is the phenomenon of post-memory. Post-memory is more than just the handing down of memory; it becomes a claim to, and appropriation of, experiences lived by ancestors. When it is enunciated and transmitted, this memory becomes a sort of inheritance, no longer an individual but a collective responsibility.[4] Transmitting memories always involves choices about what will be preserved and what will be forgotten. As time goes by, the more private memories are confronted with collective memories and institutional history. Ngungunyane's memory today remains caught up in these dynamics; the Emperor can be read as a national ghost that both haunts and inspires. He lives in the space between the silence that must be exorcised in the communities that suffered from his massacres and the demystification of those who took him as a hero. In this way, resorting to the metaphor of ghosts is a way of 'destabilising Manichean and dichotomous analyses, dismantling binaries such as present and past, memory and history, good and evil, life and death, upon which many of the narratives that make up the archive of imagination have relied'.[5]

Recognising the lacunae within past narratives and articulating these silences are first steps towards rebuilding history. The first novel written in Mozambique about Ngungunyane was *Ualalapi* (1987) by Ungulani Ba Ka Khosa. The author reconstructs the image of the last emperor of Gaza, Ngungunyane. This critical rereading of history promotes the desecration of the 'Lion of Gaza' using historical documents and proverbs from Mozambique. The polyphony of the narrative, mixing real documents and

4 Marianne Hirsch, *The Generation of Postmemory: Writing and Visual Culture after the Holocaust* (New York: Columbia University Press, 2012).

5 Inês Nascimento Rodrigues, *Espectros de Batepá: memórias e narrativas do «Massacre de 1953» em S. Tomé e Príncipe* (Porto: Afrontamento, 2018), 32.

fiction, allows the emergence of new interpretations and new identities linked to Ngungunyane.

In this chapter, I examine the presence and persistence of Ngungunyane's 'ghost' through a reading of the second volume of the trilogy *Sands of the Emperor*, in which Mia Couto chronicles the last days of the so-called Gaza State, the second biggest empire ruled by an African. Notwithstanding all the scientific material already produced on the Emperor, Couto's trilogy takes on the task of constructing a dialogue with history. Couto starts with the mystification surrounding the figure of Ngungunyane. The Portuguese portrayed the Emperor as more powerful than he really was. Their narrative was intended to demonstrate to rival colonising powers that Portugal had the military power to annihilate this African empire.

Captain Mouzinho de Albuquerque's mission represented a restitution of national pride as well as a military victory. The Portuguese success was presented as epic – an historic victory – when in fact Ngungunyane's power had dissipated due to internal conflicts, which facilitated the Portuguese 'victory'. In Mozambique, the Ngungunyane empire had profound social implications, though only affected the southern half of the country for 60 years. Within this vast territory, some reacted with devotion and submission, others with rejection.

To illustrate the complexity that surrounds this ambivalent hero, Mia Couto alternates between two narrative voices: Imani, a teenager from the Vatxopi tribe who was educated by Jesuits, and Germano de Melo, a Republican Portuguese sergeant who was deported after supporting revolts against the monarchy. In his literary representation of historical fact, Couto alternates between two ways of (re)evaluating the past: one poetic and the other bureaucratic. This mirrors his research into radically different historical sources and the process of transforming these sources into his writing. Firstly, Couto consulted hundreds of Portuguese documents about the so-called 'pacification campaigns in Mozambique'. These appear repeatedly as citations at the beginning of chapters. Secondly, Couto draws on oral sources from Mozambique – especially from the Zavala regions, home to the Vatxopi people, most affected by the Emperor's massacres. These records are extremely rich sources from which to reconstruct the transmission of oral memories. Drawing on these disparate registers,

Couto chose to write his version of this history both from the perspective of the 'winners' of the official history, the Portuguese, illustrated by the figure of Sergeant Germano, and from the perspective of the Vatxopi ethnic group, victims of the Emperor and allied to the Portuguese. Imani represents this perspective.

Stuart Hall argues that postcolonial work should bring an interest in the present and the future to bear on the question of how the past is recovered or (re)discovered.[6] Thus, cultural practices and narratives about identity, when they give their own account of the past, as Couto's work does, become themselves sites where identity is produced.[7] My goal here is to understand whether the ghost of Ngungunyane evolves from a fantasy of the past to become a part of a shared cultural present. The challenge is to cross the boundaries of reworked memory in Mia Couto's novel and to analyse how the author develops the discourses, silences and fantasies of the past to narrate history and address its ghosts.

Jo Labanyi's understanding of ghosts of history underpins this discussion. I understand post-memory in its broad sense, rather than just naming the transmission of memory, post-memory involves a claim, an appropriation of an ancestor's experience, that becomes not an individual but a collective responsibility.[8] My argument is that Ngungunyane, as he is represented in artistic work, and especially in Couto's, is already part of a shared culture. I understand Couto to be interrogating the ghost of Ngungunyane to give him a 'good death', because his death in exile, after the humiliation he suffered, allowed him to become a ghost in the popular imagination. By reworking his legacy, his heritage can become a cultural fact where myths and conflicts in various versions of history can engage in dialogue – that is, without giving credit only to one side of the story – either to the heroicity conveyed by FRELIMO or to the perversion and

6 Stuart Hall, 'Cultural Identity and Diaspora', in Stuart Hall, *Identity: Community, Culture, Difference* (London: Lawrence & Wishart, 1990) 222–237.

7 Ibid., 224.

8 Jo Labanyi, 'O reconhecimento dos fantasmas do passado: história, ética e representação', in Ana Paula Ferreira and Margarida Calafate Ribeiro, eds., *Fantasmas e fantasias imperiais no imaginário português contemporâneo* (Porto: Campo das Letras, 2003).

inhumanity described by those who suffered his massacres. Last but not least, Ngungunyane remains a ghost in popular Vatxopi imagery and reworking his legacy can solidify into a cultural fact.

Transmission of memories and writing of hi/story

> 'El olvido es una de las formas de la memoria'
> [Forgetfulness is one of the forms of memory]
>
> – Jorge Luis Borges

When invited to give a lecture on the theme of 'Literature, Identity and Memory' in Pernambuco in 2012, Mia Couto spoke about forgetfulness. His lecture drew on the events of the Mozambican Civil War, which lasted 16 years and left more than a million people dead. For the author, forgetfulness offered a way out of the traumas of the war: 'Isso foi uma estratégia para a paz. Para continuarmos a nossa caminhada sem mais Guerra' ['This was a strategy for peace. To continue our path without further war']. Though he notes the role of forgetting in the establishment of peace, Couto argued that 'a memória é um modo de ganharmos soberania sobre a nossa vida e de ser coprodutores do mundo' ['memory is a way to gain sovereignty over our lives and to be coproducers of the world']. As studies of the Shoah have shown, this apparent forgetting really registers the impossibility of articulating the trauma. Moreover, despite the apparent silence, trauma does get passed on to future generations. As the epigraph to this section puts it, forgetting is a form of memory.

We can say that the historical trauma of colonisation in Africa produced narratives full of ghosts. Official history is full of vacancies, omissions and disappearances, it is artificially continuous and often distorted. Underneath the thin layer of official history, there are stories that have been erased or silenced, leaving only their ghostly marks, and therefore destined to re-haunt the present.

For Mia Couto, people invent their constructions of the past. In his study of collective memories, the sociologist Maurice Halbwach privileges memories' social dimension. For Halbwach, as for Mia Couto, memory is a social construction, and the memory of the past is reconstructed in the present, not recovered from the past.[9] As such, when we talk about collective memory, we are talking about a present collective consciousness of the past, rather than just personal memories. But as Mia Couto explains, talking about the need to elaborate a single history for a single nation, forgetfulness is as important as memory:

> A verdade é a seguinte: esquecer não é um lapso, não é uma passiva ausência que tomba naturalmente como uma folha seca e morta. O esquecimento é, como a memória, uma fabricação, uma narrativa construída e partilhada. O que nos faz ser nação não é apenas o que juntos lembramos. Mas é sobretudo o que esquecemos e como esquecemos juntos. A literatura pode colocar a nu esse processo sem que intente exatamente denunciar ou proclamar verdades. O ficcionista sugere o seguinte: eis a minha obra, é uma ficção, uma mentira que diz que mente.[10]
>
> [The truth is this: forgetting is not a lapse, it is not a passive absence that falls naturally like a dry, dead leaf. Forgetfulness is, like memory, a fabrication, a built and shared narrative. What makes us a nation is not just what we remember together. It is above all what we forget and how we forget together. Literature can uncover this process without attempting to accurately denounce or proclaim truths. The fiction writer proposes the following: here is my work, it is a fiction, a lie that says it lies].

The study of memory and, more recently, of its transmission as postmemory, is directly related to investigations of collective identity. It is today one of the most active and interdisciplinary theoretical fields. Pierre Nora's study *Les Lieux de mémoire* (Realms of Memory), has strengthened this connection between memory studies and literary studies.[11] For Nora, the predominance of mass cultures in global society makes the role of memory

9 Maurice Halbwachs and Gérard Namer, *Les cadres sociaux de la mémoire* (Paris, France: Albin Michel, 1994).

10 Leonardo Cazes, 'Eu sou da fronteira entre culturas', *Jornal O Globo* (16 November 2015), accessed on 18 August 2018, <https://oglobo.globo.com/cultura/livros/eu-sou-da-fronteira-entre-culturas-diz-mia-couto-18058055#ixzz5I81aWPGB>

11 Pierre Nora, ed., *Les Lieux de mémoire*, Bibliothèque Illustrée Des Histoires (Paris: Gallimard, 2002).

less important today, in part because memory has been replaced by history. However, Nora points out that memory reincarnates in places where there is a sense of historical continuity.[12] In writing about Ngungunyane, Couto questions the ways a polysemic past has been crystallised into a single official version. The author is aware that school history syllabuses affect the histories told in families. Thus memory, which is produced in the present and for the present, is often endowed with a simplistic and Manichean view of history, where there are only great heroes and great traitors, and ordinary people are overlooked. In fact, ordinary people produce the past, but they have no rights to collective memory. 'Literature can bring humanity back to these infinite weavers of time',[13] says Mia Couto. In this way, the author writes a book in which historical fact matters less than the possibilities of understanding the past:

> Os fatos históricos estão ali como rochedos que dão sustento ao resto da paisagem. Os grandes momentos, as batalhas, as negociações, os chefes dos vários exércitos, esses são inspirados na história oficial. Todo o resto é invenção. E todo o resto é o mais importante, pois eu quero fazer uma história sobre os modos de invenção do passado.[14]
>
> [The historical facts are there like cliffs that bolster the rest of the landscape. The great moments, the battles, the negotiations, the heads of the various armies, these are inspired by the official history. Everything else is invention. And all the rest is the most important, because I want to make a story about ways of inventing the past.]

In addition to the war between the Portuguese and the people of Gaza, *Sands of the Emperor* treats identity and its constructions through time. The trilogy is composed of *Woman of the Ashes* (2015), *The Sword and the Spear* (2016) and *The Horizon Drinker* (2017), which ends the epic with the capture of Emperor Ngungunyane by the Portuguese. In this chapter

12 Ibid., 7.

13 Ubiratan Brasil, 'Mia Couto inicia trilogia em que reflete sobre a memória – cultura – estadão,' 18 November 2015, <https://cultura.estadao.com.br/noticias/literatura,mia-couto-inicia-trilogia-em-que-reflete-sobre-a-memoria-,10000002234>.

14 Leonardo Cazes, 'Eu sou da fronteira entre culturas', *Jornal O Globo* (16 November, 2015), accessed on 18 August 2018, <https://oglobo.globo.com/cultura/livros/eu-sou-da-fronteira-entre-culturas-diz-mia-couto-18058055#ixzz5I81aWPGB>

I deal with the second volume of the trilogy, *The Sword and the Spear*, which dramatises the end of the war. In this second book, Ngungunyane is not only talked about; he appears physically as a character. Mia Couto's mobilisation of characters that really existed through a double strategy of drawing on the extant writings and also reinventing what happened allows us to better understand both the Emperor of Gaza and the Portuguese, and to reach a more complex view than would be provided by a single perception described in a document written by a European or recorded by Mozambican oral transmission. This strategy enables Couto not only to see the Portuguese as colonisers and murderers, but also to consider all the questions surrounding their choices when invading Mozambique. Mia Couto shows how they could be perceived if more versions of the story existed.

How ghosts populate history

According to Jo Labanyi 'ghosts are, by definition, the vanquished of history … [and] always contain a sense of tragically interrupted potential … that constitutes a "bad death"'.[15] At the time of the independence struggle, Ngungunyane represented a ghost of the anticolonial fight, someone who had their life tragically interrupted by the powers of the future colonial occupation. However, he survives as a ghost in the various reappropriations of his life history – and especially by the epic narrative built by the Portuguese to ennoble their victory. Since the independence period, the memory of his 'bad death' in the Azores (following his exhibition in a human zoo, designed to humiliate a vanquished colonial 'Other') has increasingly faded. It has been replaced by the figure of an important man who illustrates a historical moment. He was re-remembered

15 Jo Labanyi, 'O reconhecimento dos fantasmas do passado: história, ética e representação', in Ana Paula Ferreira and Margarida Calafate Ribeiro, eds., *Fantasmas e fantasias imperiais no imaginário português contemporâneo*, (Porto, Portugal: Campo das Letras, 2003), 61.

as an Emperor who resisted the colonial attacks at the end of the nineteenth century and whose defeat allowed Portuguese sovereignty in the territory that is now Mozambique.

In the post-independence period, Ngungunyane became the 'symbol of forgotten potential whose achievement was frustrated.'[16] He enters the history of Mozambique as a ghost, insofar as 'the losers of history only have a place in the national narrative as ghosts or revenants'.[17] Couto revealed in an interview with the newspaper *Le Point Afrique* that people refused to talk to him when he started working with the Vatxopi tribe, out of a belief that ghosts should be left alone. The author responds: 'Mais quand les gens cherchent à oublier, ne vaut-il pas mieux réveiller les fantômes que de les laisser vous réveiller?'[18] [When people seek to forget, isn't it better to wake up the ghosts yourself rather than let them wake you up?]. Couto wasn't trying to be controversial, but showing that nation-building is forged through violent processes. The author negotiated several different pasts and built a plural history of Mozambique and Ngungunyane before writing his work.

In the literary representations of Ngungunyane, however, memory is not at stake, since ghosts are not memories. Moreover, 'memory' presupposes a narrative and, according to Labanyi, 'ghosts represent a failure in the narrative'.[19] When Ngungunyane appears in literary representations he is figured as that which 'could have been', an alternative reality embodied by art. As Derrida explains 'we do not summon the ghosts, but they insist on appearing to summon us to action'.[20] Thus, the ghost of Ngungunyane functions to mark a series of disappearances. Official history is full of gaps, omissions and disappearances; it is only artificially linear, and is often

16 Ibid., 62.

17 Ibid., 62.

18 Valérie Marin La Meslée, 'L'Histoire est pleine de mensonges et d'oublis', *Le Point Afrique*, last modified 18 June 2017, accessed 18 August 2018, <http://afrique.lepoint.fr/culture/mozambique-mia-couto-l-histoire-est-pleine-de-mensonges-et-d-oublis-18-06-2017-2136177_2256.php>.

19 Ferreira and Ribeiro, *Fantasmas e fantasias imperiais no imaginário português contemporâneo*, 64.

20 Ibid., 67.

distorted. Underneath the thin layer of official history, there are stories that have been erased or silenced, leaving only their ghostly marks, purposefully reactivated for political purposes. The return of independence leaders' ghosts such as Patrice Lumumba, Ruben Um Nyobe, Amílcar Cabral, Thomas Sankara, Nkwame Nkrumah or Sékou Touré, many of whom were murdered between 1960 and the beginning of 1990, allows us to move beyond silenced histories of the past and towards shared cultures of the present. It is part of a postcolonial narrative, which used fabricated heroes as a tool for national unification, and as tropes to construct singular histories in order to create a sense of belonging for the people.

Mia Couto recalls, in an initial note, that some believe that the bones Portugal returned to Mozambique in 1985 are actually just sand. It is this sand that gives the trilogy its name because, as Couto affirms, sand is a metaphor for empire. 'É nela, como na terra, que se guarda a memória do que fomos e do que somos'[21] [It is on it [the sand], as on earth, that we keep the memory of what we were and what we are].

Ngungunyane

> Imperador eterno me sonhei. Mas terei o destino dos escravos [...] Os meus ossos irão morar para além do mar. E de mim ninguém mais terá lembrança. O esquecimento é o único modo de morrer para sempre. E será ainda pior: os que de mim mais se lembrarem serão os que nunca me quiseram bem.[22]
> [I dreamed of myself as an eternal Emperor. But I will suffer the fate of the slaves [...] My bones will live beyond the sea. And no one will remember me any more. Forgetting is the only way to die forever. And it will be even worse: those who remember me the most will be those who never loved me].

21 Marcos Borga, 'Visão Mia Couto, novo romance, novos desafios', *Jornal Visão* (10 October 2015), <http://visao.sapo.pt/jornaldeletras/letras/2015-10-21-Mia-Couto-novo-romance-novos-desafios>.

22 Mia Couto, *As Areias do Imperador*, 331.

There are several theories to explain the presence of recurrent ghosts in contemporary narratives of the past. Many critics assert they represent a questioning of the official narrative and represent spectral histories full of discontinuities and absences. Ghosts arise as a response to the need to create new versions of the past, where the omissions of official histories are not repeated, and where the victims of modernity do not disappear from the historical record.

From the example of Ngungunyane we can note how useful the trope of ghosts of history is in analysing the generational transmissions of colonisation and decolonisation in Africa. In the sentence that Mia Couto attributes to Ngungunyane, which appears in the opening of this section, we see the Emperor's clear-sightedness about himself and his future. In the book, Couto represents Ngungunyane as aware of his own fragility and of the ways he was losing territories and the war to the Portuguese. The foresightedness of his words – Couto's construction – brings into view the Emperor's lucidity with regards to his destiny.

Mia Couto's interest in the Emperor of Gaza is based on questions of reconstructing the past and in constructing collective memories. According to the author, 'we are faced with two historical lies invented in the service of political interests'. As in Ngungunyane's prophecy, Couto uses the perspectives of the Emperor's opponents, the Vatxopi and the Portuguese. In Couto's story, Ngungunyane's allies already appear as 'traitors'. They use their closeness to the Emperor to scare rather than to support him and they celebrate his capture. Stuart Hall argues that in order to understand cultural identity one must focus on 'becoming rather than being' to avoid falling into a notion of accepted or pre-constructed identity.[23] In Mia Couto's book, it is precisely the becoming of the Emperor's image that is in question: between official documents and creative fiction, Mia Couto reanimates ghosts in order to construct a collective identity in relation (or not) to a collective memory of Ngungunyane. This is postmemorial work, which, as Marianne Hirsch states, 'strives to reactivate and re-embody more distant political and cultural memorial structures

23 Stuart Hall, 'Introduction: Who Needs "Identity"?,' in *Questions of Cultural Identity*, ed. Stuart Hall and Paul du Gay (London: Sage Publications, 1996), 4.

by reinvesting them with individual and familial forms of mediation and aesthetic expression.'[24]

Ghosts, as the incarnation of the past in the present, destabilise accepted notions of history, of individual reality, as well as the limits that define them. Ghosts remind us that we need to face our past if we are to advance and build a better future. The reappearance of ghosts in the history of several African countries is closely related to the way in which colonialism erased countries' pasts as though their history began with colonialism. The return of ghosts in current narratives is a symptom of a collective longing to address this past, but at the same time offers the possibility of rectification, recognition, and reparation. In this way Ngungunyane represents the shadows of a continental history that still waits to be recovered, resolved and repaired.

In the first book of Couto's trilogy, we hear about the Emperor only via the actions of his armies. It is only in the last third of the second volume that we are confronted with the character in the flesh. Here, I focus on the second book to better understand how his image is perceived and how his reputation circulates. Then, I will analyse Couto's strategies for developing the character when he physically appears as a character.

Mia Couto mixes historical writings with the oral histories he has collected. As in many of his novels, each chapter is preceded by a quotation. In *Sands of the Emperor*, historical texts are mixed with proverbial sayings, either real or inspired by the philosophy of each character or village. In this article I will focus on Portuguese written sources and perspectives rather than on African historical (oral) sources, since in the novel there are more elements to contest the European historical point of view than the African.

The first mention of Emperor Ngungunyane in the second book of the trilogy comes as early as Chapter 6, in the second letter of Lieutenant Ayres de Ornelas. Thanks to a report written by Colonel José Justino Teixeira Botelho, in the 1921 *Historia Militar e Política dos Portugueses em Moçambique de 1883 aos Nossos Dias* [*Military History and Politics of the Portuguese in Mozambique from 1883 to The Present Day*], we know that the Portuguese considered themselves superior to the African army, the latter's

24 Hirsch, *The Generation of Postmemory*, 11.

audacity notwithstanding.[25] When someone from the Gungunhane kraal comes to say that he has witnessed 'uma parada de quinze mil guerreiros de aspeto imponente'[26] [a parade of fifteen thousand warriors of imposing appearance], the Colonel dismisses this army as an armed mob and judges the Africans mere 'savages'. This account shows the disdain in which the military commanders held Ngungunyane's army.

In his 1934 book *Colectânea das suas principais obras militares e coloniais, vol 1* [*Collection of principal military and colonial works, vol 1*], Lieutenant Aires de Ornelas (who also appears in Couto's fiction), reveals that no one spoke of the colonial campaigns in the military school – whether of strategies or opponents.[27] Ayres' account inspires Couto to choose him as a narrative informant of the Portuguese mission. In the novel, his letters show the apparent lack of interest that both he and General Germano de Almeida have in the colonial campaign in Mozambique.

By contrast, commander Mouzinho de Albuquerque (who also appears in both the real story and the fiction) is fully engaged in the fight against Ngungunyane: 'percebi que Gungunhane ainda era muito temido e respeitado, devido em parte às mortes que todos os dias mandava fazer, e, por isso, fiz o possível por inspirar um terror igual ao que espalhava em torno de si o régulo Vátua'.[28] ['I realised that Gungunhane was still very much feared and respected, due in part to the deaths he ordered every day and so I did what I could to inspire a terror equal to what the little Vátuan chief sprinkled around him']. This passage from a real piece of writing appears as a quotation in one of Lieutenant Ayres' letters. In this letter he justifies the Portuguese military's new *modus operandi*: though victory had been part of their strategy, it hadn't been recognised by their African opponents. They, he says, only accept the end of the battle with fire and destruction. Ngungunyane inspired respect through his dictatorship of

25 José Justino Teixeira Botelho, *História militar e política dos portugueses em Moçambique: de 1833 aos nossos dias* (Lisbon: Centro Tip. Colonial, 1936).

26 Couto, *As Areias do Imperador*, 37.

27 Aires de Ornelas, *Colectânea das suas principais obras militares e coloniais, vol 1* (Lisbon: Divisão de Publicações e Biblioteca, Agência Geral das Colónias, 1934–1936).

28 Couto, *As areias do imperador*, 92.

fear and death – and the Portuguese too began to fight in that way. But the lieutenant does not agree with Mouzinho's orders, because the destruction left after a victory is not a good outcome.

In that same letter, in Chapter 30, Ayres explains that General Germano de Almeida's disobedience to his orders made him 'perceber melhor as minhas próprias funções' [better aware of my own functions].[29] It gives rise to several issues that call into question what the Portuguese really know about the Africans and about the war in which they are involved: 'ninguém senão nós chamamos Vátuas aos Vanguni. Ninguém mais usa o termo "Estado de Gaza". Como lhe chamam os próprios cafres?'[30] [No one else but us calls the Vanguni Vátuas. No one else uses the term 'Gaza State'. What do the kaffirs themselves call it?].

Crucially, Lieutenant Ayres readopts the etymology used by the Vanguni to identify Ngungunyane, *nkossi*: 'Com a mesma palavra designam Deus'[31] [the same word they use to designate God]. Ayres demonstrates that a people's understanding of what an Emperor is shapes their reaction to Ngungunyane, who is understood as a figure with divine authority to punish and reward. Ayres concludes, 'A nossa guerra não tem apenas uma dimensão militar. É uma guerra religiosa'[32] [Our war is not just military. It's a religious war]. As General Germano de Almeida insisted in his earlier letters: 'se queremos derrotar os africanos teremos que os conhecer melhor, teremos que penetrar no seu mundo e viver entre esses outros povos'[33] [if we want to defeat the Africans we will have to know them better, we will have to penetrate their world and live among these other peoples]. Ayres emphasises that this is precisely the Africans' strategy, who already speak Portuguese and understand how Europeans live and organise themselves. Ayres sees how unprepared the Portuguese were when they arrived in Africa to deal with an enemy in a foreign territory, and that the Africans 'espalharam pelo sertão africano as notícias do nosso poder, mas sobretudo a das nossas

29 Ibid., 295.
30 Ibid., 296.
31 Ibid., 296.
32 Ibid., 296.
33 Ibid., 297.

fraquezas'[34] [spread the news of our power in the African backlands, but especially of our weaknesses].

In that sense, Father Rudolfo Fernandes confirms the Africans' strategy when he reveals that 'Gungunhane é o homem mais cosmopolita que conheço: fala diversas línguas, negoceia com várias nações'[35] [Gungunhane is the most cosmopolitan man I know: he speaks several languages, he deals with several nations]. The Portuguese understand the political impact of the *nkossi*, as revealed in the Marques Geraldes *Report* of 1888: 'Sente-se ao chegar próximo de Gungunhane uma simpatia inexplicável ... encontra-se nele um conjunto de atrativos que nos predispõem logo a seu favor' [You feel an inexplicable sympathy when you get close to Gungunhane ... you feel a set of attractive qualities that predispose us to him][36] At the end of this account Geraldes points out that despite his charms, Ngungunyane 'tem uma vontade de ferro, que não se dobra por cousa alguma'[37] [has an iron will, which does not bend for anything]. This is a political advantage: knowing how to please everyone at the same time as getting your way.

In a second key moment in the book, perhaps a gloss on the official story, Ngungunyane's mother appears. She reminds the Portuguese leaders that part of the Portuguese promises were never fulfilled. She notes that the same was true on the African side and concludes that 'temos memória é para esquecer as nossas culpas'[38] [we remember in order to forget our faults]. She presents a plan to save Portuguese honour and Ngungunyane's life. Through Impibekezane's action, Couto shows us how the situation was perceived: Ngungunyane's days were numbered; he was militarily weakened and losing support. Doing a deal was the best option. At the same time, to avoid further war and destruction, and perhaps also to avoid dishonouring the Portuguese army, she proposes a deal which would allow the Portuguese to appear as the sole victors in the eyes of the world: 'Os únicos que não reconheceriam nunca essa vitória seriam os vencidos. E assim ao

34 Ibid., 297.
35 Ibid., 283.
36 Ibid., 293.
37 Ibid., 293.
38 Ibid., 115.

longo dos séculos festejariam, de outro modo, seu triunfo'[39] [The only ones who would never recognise this victory were the losers. And so over the centuries they celebrated their triumph]. This sentence from Germano de Almeida's letter to Lieutenant Ayres summarises what would enter into history – the Portuguese victory; and what would be forgotten – the fact that this was an agreement between Impibekezane and the Portuguese military – which was hardly a warlike strategy.

The Swiss missionaries, who have a hospital in Sana Benene, are also significant figures. Hospitals and doctors represent neutral territory in the battle. Several confessions pass through doctors, such as Ngungunyane's, who explains intimate episodes of his past. The doctor, a specialist in hypnosis, wonders: 'como hipnotizar alguém que não só fala uma outra língua como para quem voar e sonhar são um mesmo verbo' [how can I hypnotise someone who not only speaks another language but also for whom 'fly' and 'dream' are one and the same verb?]. Ngungunyane says that he only thinks when he dreams, 'e não sei quem sou quando sonho'[40] [and I do not know who I am when I dream]. Here Mia Couto introduces Ngungunyane's part in the murder of his brother, the heir to the throne. Ngungunyane reveals his guilt when he says he only obeyed orders 'e esse foi o meu maior erro'[41] [and that was my biggest mistake]. He suggests it is no longer he who dreams when he sleeps: 'eu durmo e o meu irmão sonha dentro de mim'[42] [I sleep and my brother dreams inside me]. To appease his pain, the doctor reassures him that his act was to protect Zixaxa, an Emperor who escaped from the Portuguese, and that this gesture of loyalty counterbalances his sins. Ngungunyane replies that Zixaxa is not actually protected, but imprisoned, in Ngungunyane's realm: he is his future adversary. Mia Couto uses the neutral territory of the hospital and the trope of a passive listener to inform readers about Ngungunyane's choices and actions. Imani hears and reports the consultation, concluding that 'o grande mendigo era o imperador' [the great beggar was the Emperor], because he was always

39 Ibid., 116.
40 Ibid., 326.
41 Ibid., 327.
42 Ibid., 327.

asking for things and needing people.[43] Couto, then, uses this moment to show the fragility of the empire of Gaza.

Imani subsequently introduces herself to Ngungunyane as a messenger sent by Vuiaze, the forbidden lover of the Gazan king, for 'um amor tão ardente poderia distrair o futuro governante' [such ardent love could distract the future ruler].[44] The king had a son with Vuiaze, Godido, but one day Vuiaze died, and her body disappeared. Therefore, the king asserts that 'confio mais no álcool que me é oferecido pelo meu inimigo do que nas bebidas que me servem os familiares'[45] [I trust more in the alcohol my enemies offer me than in the drinks my relatives serve]. Ngungunyane is preoccupied by the notion of being surrounded by disloyal people with their own interests. When Imani offers herself as a new wife, he takes the request with suspicion, asking his counsellors' opinion. In fact, Imani marrying the king is part of an assassination plot drawn up by her father: 'Não a mando para ser esposa. Vai lá para ser viúva'[46] [I'm not sending her there to be a wife. I'm sending her there to be a widow].

The undoing of the Emperor comes in Chapter 44, in the form of a letter from Germano de Melo.[47] In it we learn that the Portuguese, for fear of losing the glory of earlier battles won, ask that the army call off their mission to capture Ngungunyane. But Germano is late to the scene. The Emperor is already in the hands of his opponents, and everything happens surprisingly easily. Mia Couto opens the chapter with actual documents from Mouzinho de Albuquerque's report. 'Obriguei-o então à força a sentar-se no chão (cousa que elle nunca fazia), dizendo que ele já não era régulo dos Manguins mas um matonga como qualquer outro'[48] [I forced him to sit on the floor (which he never did), saying that he was no longer a manguins ruler but a matonga like all the rest]. When a group of women walks past Germano, they comment: 'Gugunhane sentou no chão! Os portugueses já o têm amarrado'[49] [Gungunhane sat on the floor! The Portuguese have tied

43 Ibid., 328.
44 Ibid., 346.
45 Ibid., 347.
46 Ibid., 349.
47 Ibid., 441.
48 Ibid., 442.
49 Ibid., 444.

him already]. Another group of people sing 'Abutre, abutre, vai-te embora, abutre. Nunca mais assaltarás nossas galinhas'[50] [Vulture, vulture, go away, vulture. You shall no more assail our hens].

In his book *Memories* (1985), the Mozambican writer Raúl Bernardo Honwana (1905–1994) says: 'Nunca se conseguiu perceber bem o verdadeiro sentimento dos nguni em relação ao Gugunhane … aquela multidão gritou o seguinte: Vai-te embora, seu abutre, que dizimas as galinhas'[51] [The true feeling of the Nguni in relation to Gungunhane was never well understood … That multitude shouted: Be gone, you vulture, you who slaughter the chickens]. Mia Couto describes the moment of departure as 'uma tempestade de insultos (…) dirigida a Ngungunyane, esse mesmo rei que durante anos tinham idolatrado'[52] [a storm of insults (…) directed at Ngungunyane, the same king who had been idolised for years].

Imani, in spite of trying to assassinate the king on the way to the sea, ends up falling into her father's trap: she is sent into exile along with her husband the Emperor, his opponent Zixaxa, and his several wives: 'naquele barco viajavam não apenas pessoas diversas mas mundos em colisão'[53] [not just different people but colliding worlds travelled in that boat]. The Portuguese treated all Africans the same, ignoring internal conflicts or 'colliding worlds'. This concludes the second volume of the trilogy.

Final remarks

My goal here has been to analyse how Mia Couto crosses the boundaries of how memory is re-elaborated, especially when contesting European written sources. I do so to understand how he develops the discourses, silences and fantasies of the past in order to narrate history by confronting

50 Ibid., 445.
51 Raul Honwana, *Memorias* (Maputo, Mozambique: Edições Asa, 1989), 449.
52 Couto, *As Areias do Imperador*, 458.
53 Ibid., 460.

history's ghosts and the mythologising of the Gazan king. In this sense, as Avery Gordon argues,

> writing ghost stories … not only repair[s] representational mistakes, but also strive[s] to understand the conditions under which a memory was produced in the first place, toward a counter memory, for the future.[54]

Mia Couto uses Ngungunyane and his stories as an instrument of mediation. He shows how ghosts are ambiguous and hard to pin down, which complicates the ways that past fantasies can evolve into shared cultures in the present. In confronting the Vatxopi people with memories that are, given their fear of waking ghosts, 'unthinkable', Couto shows that the best way forward is to give the ghost a good death so that it can no longer cause terror. This is a storyteller's logic. In his version of the story, Mia Couto brings out the humanity of the Emperor of Gaza, a character feared for his massacres against the Vatxopi; purposefully portrayed by the Portuguese as a bloodthirsty and powerful adversary; and remembered by the Mozambican leaders and liberation movements as a true resister of colonisation.

Using the voices of Ngungunyane's enemies, the Portuguese and the Vatxopi, Couto presents the Emperor as an imposing presence in the territory but one who, despite instilling fear and terror, was also a very cosmopolitan figure. The Emperor appears as a passionate person, who fell in love, suffered for love and who liked to drink port wine.

More than on the myths constructed (and under construction) around Ngungunyane, Couto builds his accounts on several small stories. As we have seen, the fragments that illustrate each chapter develop our impression of the Emperor, make us question what war is, evaluate the fragility of empires, become aware of the way language shapes us. The fictional military letters show that there is a great semantic gap between an 'emperor' and a '*nkossi*.' Indeed, we also see a gap in the double spelling of the Emperor's name throughout the book: in Portuguese official documents, his name is written according to Portuguese norms and pronunciation, while in

54 Avery Gordon, *Ghostly Matters Haunting and the Sociological Imagination* (Minnesota: University of Minnesota Press, 2008), 22.

the rest of the story, African norms dominate. I have followed that logic in this chapter.

The third volume presents avenues for further investigating the image of the Emperor after he is dethroned and exiled. If in that book Ngungunyane becomes a trophy and dies in exile, in the first two books, Ngungunyane's late entrance into the narrative make him a spectral character as well, even when he is alive. It is in the second book that Couto centrally develops Ngungunyane's dichotomies that shed light on the conflicting position he evokes in the popular imagination. The characters' experiences in relation to Ngungunyane, along with the historical documents that underpin the text, allow us to explore the many layers of this mythical figure.

Though it was initially the Mozambican leaders who, for political reasons, turned Ngungunyane into a national hero, the later vandalism of his statue was a reaction to the reappearance of a ghost – and even to the perceived legitimacy of FRELIMO. This ambivalence around the figure of Ngungunyane persists in contestations of the Mozambican narrative. Waking this ghost up enables Couto to approach the historical dimension of the character from a bi-national perspective, as well as to assess his political value as a national hero. More than just telling his version of the story, Couto illustrates how various versions of history can overlap or complement each other and be adapted to serve political discourses. Finally, in his trilogy, Mia Couto reveals that history is living and that it is built in consonance with the present.

Works cited

Borga, Marcos. 'Visão Mia Couto, novo romance, novos desafios.' *Jornal Visão* (10 October 2015). Accessed 18 August 2018. <http://visao.sapo.pt/jornaldeletras/letras/2015-10-21-Mia-Couto-novo-romance-novos-desafios>.

Botelho, José Justino Teixeira. *História militar e política dos Portugueses em Moçambique: de 1833 aos nossos dias*. Lisbon: Centro Tip. Colonial, 1936.

Brasil, Ubiratan. 'Mia Couto inicia trilogia em Qque reflete sobre a memória – cultura – estadão.' (18 November 2015). Accessed 18 August 2018. <https://

cultura.estadao.com.br/noticias/literatura,mia-couto-inicia-trilogia-em-que-reflete-sobre-a-memoria-,10000002234>.

Cazes, Leonardo. Entrevista a Mia Couto: 'Eu sou da fronteira entre culturas'. *Jornal O Globo* (16 November 2015). Accessed 18 August 2018. <https://oglobo.globo.com/cultura/livros/eu-sou-da-fronteira-entre-culturas-diz-mia-couto-18058055#ixzz5I81aWPGB>.

Couto, Mia. *As Areias do Imperador: Uma Trilogia Moçambicana. Livro Dois, A Espada e a Azagaia*. Alfragide, Portugal: Caminho, 2016.

Ferreira, Ana Paula, and Margarida Calafate Ribeiro, eds. *Fantasmas e fantasias imperiais no imaginário português contemporâneo*. Porto: Campo das Letras, 2003.

Gordon, Avery. *Ghostly Matters Haunting and the Sociological Imagination*. Minnesota: University of Minnesota Press, 2008.

Halbwachs, Maurice, and Gérard Namer. *Les cadres sociaux de la mémoire*. Paris, France: Albin Michel, 1994.

Hall, Stuart. 'Cultural Identity And Diaspora.' In Stuart Hall, *Identity: Community, Culture, Difference*, 222–237. London: Lawrence & Wishart, 1990.

Hall, Stuart, and Paul du Gay, eds. *Questions of Cultural Identity*. London: Sage Publications, 1996.

Hirsch, Marianne. *The Generation of Postmemory: Writing and Visual Culture after the Holocaust*. New York: Columbia University Press, 2012.

Honwana, Raul Bernardo Manuel. *Memorias*. Maputo: Mozambique: Edições Asa, 1989.

Labanyi, Jo. 'O Reconhecimento dos Fantasmas do Passado: História, Ética e Representação'. In *Fantasmas e Fantasias Imperiais no Imaginário Português Contemporâneo*, edited by Ana Paula Ferreira and Margarida Calafate Ribeiro, 59–68. Porto, Portugal: Campo das Letras, 2003.

La Meslée, Valérie Marin. 'L'Histoire est pleine de mensonges et d'oublis.' *Le Point Afrique* (18 June 2017). Accessed 12 July 2018. <http://afrique.lepoint.fr/culture/mozambique-mia-couto-l-histoire-est-pleine-de-mensonges-et-d-oublis-18-06-2017-2136177_2256.php>.

Nora, Pierre. 'Between Memory and History: Les Lieux de Mémoire.' *Representations* 26 (1989): 7–25.

Ornelas, Aires de. *Colectânea das suas principais obras militares e coloniais, vol 1*. Lisbon: Divisão de Publicações e Biblioteca, Agência Geral das Colónias, 1934–1936.

Rodrigues, Inês Nascimento. *Espectros de Batepá: Memórias e Narrativas do "Massacre de 1953" em S. Tomé e Príncipe*. Porto: Afrontamento, 2018.

PART III

Mixing Wor(l)ds

KRISTIAN VAN HAESENDONCK

9 An Interview with Mia Couto[1]

KVH: In recent decades, the Caribbean has produced a discourse on Creole and creoleness, two concepts that were promoted by intellectuals and writers from various parts of the Caribbean (such as Stuart Hall, Kamau Brathwaite, António Benítez Rojo, Edouard Glissant and the group of *Créolistes* from Martinique (Chamoiseau, Bernabé and Confiant). One of the most discussed texts [they produced] was *In Praise of Creoleness* (*Éloge de la créolité*). In spite of the similar processes that took place in the various parts of Lusophone Africa (Cape Verde, São Tomé and Príncipe, Guinea Buissau), there is – not that I know – any discourse about African Creole or 'Creoleness' crystallised in manifestos or other texts. However, in your essays you insist very much on processes of cultural mixing (*mestiçagem*). To what extent are these processes in Mozambique, in your view, comparable with Caribbean creolisation and with those African societies that are explicitly known as 'Creole' or 'creolised' (Cape Verde, São Tomé and Príncipe, Guinea Buissau)?

MC: This is not a topic that I've thought about very much but I think that the difference [between Mozambique and the Caribbean] is to be found in history, in Genesis. The Caribbean is a place of arrival and mixing, one of the main stages of the African diaspora, of racial mixing and the mixing of histories, which is not so much the case of Mozambique. For example, Mozambique is a place of departure, but not so much a place of arrival, only in the sense that the Europeans who arrived had very little influence, mixing here was very ephemeral and very limited. The only place in Mozambique in which this process of *mestiçagem* – of mixing in the

1 This interview was undertaken at the *Fundação Fernando Leite Couto*, Maputo, on 25 July 2016. I am indebted to Flávia das Neves Horácio for transcribing the recording of this interview.

genetic and cultural sense – happened was in the Zambezi Valley, close to the region of Inhambane. These were geographically speaking very restricted phenomena and were not sufficiently intense to produce a phenomenon of creolisation, of linguistic or cultural mixing. So I guess it was not possible to expect that in Mozambique there would be the same kind of claim; on top of that there was a certain resistance because the underlying idea was to make a racial claim, meaning that history was so mixed up with the denial of race, of culture, that it was thought to be unique; [there was] a great urgency to answer with a common voice, without distinguishing between Mozambique's different internal histories and cultures [...] Not even from the point of view of Mozambique's inner land was there a historical space for internal mixing, starting with FRELIMO. The internal processes of migratory movements were also very limited. I'm not even talking about different races: Mozambicans of black origin, therefore 99% of the population of Mozambicans, were not within [the current territory called] Mozambique. They had migrated to South Africa, to Malawi, to Rhodesia (present-day Zimbabwe) and that's where they created, for the first time, a kind of *lingua franca*. These internal differences mingled for the first time in songs and along small cultural circuits. So, I think it's a whole different history compared to those island formations [in the Caribbean], even though Mozambique was an 'island' in a very different way: It was an 'island' that needed a unified response against what was coming from the outside.

KVH: Continuing with your colleagues from the Caribbean, Edouard Glissant wrote that the contemporary world (Chaos Monde, 'Chaos-World'), is a creolising archipelago: around the world emerge new cultural islands that connect with one another, something which is even happening in Europe: The old continent is, he claims, also subject to a process of creolisation, in spite of the many atavisms that threaten its unity. Would you agree with Glissant's view, or do you believe, from an 'African' perspective, that he is perhaps too optimistic? Do cultural (Caribbean and African) processes of *mestiçagem* foreshadow the fate of our planet?

MC: This is a trend that I think is present in a continuous way. We only think of the most recent part of history, but [compared to] what we call *pre-history* – that is the great history of our species – this small piece [of history] that we promote, history in its present condition is very recent. We have hundreds of thousands of years in which we were a history that was deeply mixed; a history of exchanges, of travels, of these rhizomes that were created. We have common origins that are being forgotten, but I think that in recent times this tendency has become more obvious, it is part of our own survival, of our own … let's call it an 'essence', something that we don't have.

KVH: … an essence?

MC: … an essence which we don't have. We absorb this great diversity, but now the tendency is to reverse all this because of circumstances, because of fear, because of the military, political, religious tensions that have been created, we establish frontiers and build fortresses and look at each other.

KVH: … 'fortress Europe', for instance?

MC: Yes, Europe, for example, but also elsewhere. Africa also closed itself off, and I didn't even mention other worlds such as the Middle East, the Islamic world. There's a tendency to close doors.

KVH: In *Pensatempos* you wrote that Europe 'seeks essences instead of processes'. Glissant said, in a similar fashion, that Europe is the victim of its own atavisms: The eternal return to the national founding myths, contrary to so-called 'composite' cultures (like the Caribbean, and perhaps African cultures as well), which are open to impurity and cultural contagion. In view of the recent migratory flows to Europe, as well as the self-defence reaction and the predictable tilting to rightwing politics in various European countries, is Europe at risk of imploding?

MC: The end of Europe would be too much Europe, only in the sense of considering [itself] a pure centre, an entity that forgot about its own origin, its own history. I think that this is the result of this manufacturing of fear that is a very recent but very efficient thing … it's a theme that has been chasing me forever, since fear catalyses these processes of closure [to the outside world]. Suddenly, one must have a unique identity. For example, we forget that the Muslim presence in Europe is ancient, it is endogenous. It comes from outside Europe. And suddenly, it seems that the World order determined that Europeans were all one single thing. As if the nature of Europe were only one thing, of a different nature: a single religion, a single race, a single cultural identity.

KVH: And a monolinguism as well, perhaps?

MC: A monolinguism indeed. Europe has forgotten about its own history, its diversity, and now calls for this fear, which is fabricated. It is a political manipulation that leads to mixing up on the one hand a threat that is military and political, and a religious threat, a threat of civilisation, on the other hand. There is a whole smoke screen that has been created to serve political interests.

KVH: Cuban writer Antonio Benítez Rojo envisions the Caribbean as a non-apocalyptic space: Cubans solve problems 'in a certain way'. To illustrate his point, Benítez Rojo draws on the image of two women walking below his Havana balcony *de cierta manera*, in a 'certain' elegant, yet undescribable way; their cadence cannot be captured in words, he says. In Lusophone African literature, the theme of the apocalypse enjoys an important presence. I think of works such as Pepetela's *O quase fim do mundo*, or *Vento do Apocalípse*, by your colleague Paula Chiziane, or your own novel *Jesusalém* [translated by David Brookshaw as *The Tuner of Silences*]. The apocalypse, despite becoming a recurrent theme, is a twisted, or reflected end-of-the-world: one could say, approaching Benítez Rojo, that your characters survive 'in a certain way' (for example Mwanito in *Jesusalém*). Is it possible to imagine postcolonial Africa as a non-apocalyptic space? Or is Africa doomed to drag along the shadows of its past?

MC: I think there is one thing I didn't say before that is important to mention here. There were geographic spaces such as Cuba (and the Caribbean in general), such as a part of Brazil, in which creolisation – the possibility to syncretise languages – happened. It happened, because something deeper happened, which was religious syncretism. That's a lot deeper and allows for a language afterwards. So let's say, language is Creole, it is mixed, because the gods have been mixed, and this is very clear in Cuba and it clearly happened throughout Brazil. Suddenly, the boundary between one's own gods and other deities becomes fuzzy and this didn't happen here in Mozambique. It succeeded at a cosmetic level, but Mozambicans predominantly continue to live a certain duality; it's a reality which allows me to attend, for instance, an African ancient religious ceremony in the morning, and in the afternoon or evening I can do something else or go somewhere else. While I can cross borders, I don't encounter any great religious fusion.

I always propose that, in order to understand these historical and social processes, we should not *chercher la femme* [look for the cause of the problem], but [instead] search for the sacred, the divine element which is sometimes not completely visible. I think that in Mozambique the idea that there is an 'end-of-the-world' pursues us because as a matter of fact the world's ending is always imminent; there's always an end of *a* world, of a particular world. We had the end of the colonial world, of the world of socialism, for example. There have been several 'ends-of-the-world', several apocalypses that followed one another. People live in the anguish that their world, the traditional one with its rural values is close to an abyss; that it is being pushed to a timeless place. I think that this is not a literary issue. It is an experience that is not completely dramatic because people always have a great ability to have a foot on each side of the world. So, even there, in my novel *Jesusalém* there is an idea that writing – and this idea already appears in *Terra Somnâmbula* – can be a means of salvation, of building a bridge between a dying world and another one that's being born. So there are transitional processes in Mozambique that are experienced in a painful and intensely tragic way but I think the expression of this is not sad. It's conflictive because people also have a certain religious precept … an experience which triggers my anxiety, but it cannot be expressed because it would summon the negative gods, the negative forces. So, even if I'm crying within myself, even though I'm being torn apart on the inside, I'm always happy.

KVH: … Cubans have an expression for this: 'Here I am, screwed but happy' (aquí estoy, jodido pero feliz)…

MC: [*laughs*] It's exactly the same thing!

KVH: I would like to speak a bit of the border characters in your novels: characters living on an existential (and geographic) border and trying, in my view, to heal their wounds in unlikely circumstances. Possessed by some kind of madness, they are, in my view, not only *damnés de la terre* to use Fanon's expression; sometimes their insanity appears as a positive or healthy phenomenon, remembering the madness that we also find in a novel such as *The Kingdom of the Casuarinas* [*O Reino das Casuarinas*] by Angolan writer José Luis Mendonça. Madness, hysteria, paranoia, can they be saviours in a disenchanted world? Or is madness perhaps a defensive mechanism in a perverse symbolic order, as Slavoj Žižek would put it?

MC: Yes, absolutely. I think you need to authorise those little states of craziness in order not to become truly mad – mad in the pathological sense. Madness is felt here like something that, in order to understand these processes, which are very engaging, requires that you stay on the sidelines. If you're locked up inside madness, completely inside, if you live it with both feet on the same side of reality, you really go crazy; you're excluded from the very possibility of being a subject, because here we are talking about citizenship. Citizenship always has to be plural … citizenship in the sense of modernity, of being a historical subject of the process of nation building, but at the same time, it is necessary not to lose balance between modernity's processes of construction and reconstruction of the other identities that people have. A person can say, 'I am Mozambican', and at the same time feel that he or she belongs to this or that ethnicity. Thus, twenty years before the independence of Mozambique, there was an artificial imposition, it was almost forbidden to say, 'I am two things'. One wasn't allowed to say he or she belongs to a certain ethnicity. Talking about your ethnicity, race or religion was forbidden. But that situation didn't resolve anything, it simply postponed the creation of a space for self-affirmation, which, when that space finally appeared, emerged forcefully.

KVH: In your novels several characters experience what we might call a process of 'Africanisation' (for instance the character Marta, the Portuguese woman in *Jesusalém*; or the UN official in *The Last Flight of the Flamingo*). Here again, I would like to use the term creolisation, or rather 'reverse creolisation': the white European is transformed as soon as she/he enters into contact with African culture; the character takes on a new identity. It supposes an inversion of classical creolisation, which originates in slavery: the African taken to the new world, forced to reinvent his or her identity after clashing with his master, a clash between coloniser and colonised. Can we imagine your books as conflictive 'contact zones' where cultural impurity is somehow celebrated?

MC: Yes, indeed. That's my intention, but I don't know if I will succeed in this project. It's my intention to show that these exchange processes are always mutual, even in the case of the Portuguese language, which is already a deeply mixed language (*linguagem mestiçada*). I think the Portuguese themselves have no idea how much their language is made of elements that are, for example, African. When these linguistic or religious identities travel, or whatever [happens to them], and they think they will transform the other, they are already deeply creolised, mixed.

KVH: The term 'Creole' originally referred to the children of Spanish Europeans (settlers) who settled in the New World and who created a new culture ... To a certain extent your condition is perhaps comparable: as the son of Portuguese immigrants to Africa, you invent a new language, a Mozambican 'Africanised' Portuguese ... Where did this desire to (re) invent Portuguese through literature come from?

MC: The Portuguese language was already there. When I started telling these stories, I had no sense of a mission, in the sense of 'I'm going to do this because of that ...', some kind of political or social project. I wanted to tell stories and I realised that to tell those stories I could not use standard Portuguese. I had to abandon it. But it wasn't completely invented. I mean, I invented words, yes, they're mine. They were invented in a river, on a treadmill, as part of a social process that was happening around me. Mozambicans use Portuguese in their own way, they recreate it, transform it and mix it with their indigenous languages. Thus there was a very rich process that helped me; I don't have the merit of having started thinking of this possibility by myself. It was right there. I've just used that privilege.

KVH: I would like to talk a bit of this Lusophone linguistic community that we refer to as *Lusofonia* as well as similar *-fonias* (the French-speaking community called *Francophonie*, for instance). The Caribbean is divided into several linguistic areas linking each island and territory to a European metropolis (or the U.S. in the case of Puerto Rico). Glissant speaks of the 'Balkanisation' of the Caribbean. On the one hand, *Lusofonía* is a linguistic community (organised politically as CPLP or *Comunidade dos Países de Língua Portuguesa* [Community of Portuguese Language Countries]) that connects the various African Lusophone countries in a kind of linguistic archipelago. On the other hand, *Lusofonía* is also, like *Francophonie*, clearly a colonial construct, in the sense that it has its origin in Portuguese colonialism and its ideological tool of 'Lusotropicalismo'. As a Mozambican writer, how do you deal with this double inheritance?

MC: This is not something I'm worried about. The only Lusophone community (*Lusofonía*) that exists for me is the one that is constructed unintentionally, without a project. History built it as if it were a side effect of another project that grew over time. I do not see that the CPLP or any other organisation has helped in a process that was born for other, historical reasons. That is, there are some who created this organisation to take political advantage, and in the beginning Mozambique reacted in a very nervous way towards this project – and I think that was the correct reaction. We didn't create that project. It was a project that has a neocolonial conception. It is a project that places us apart as a 'family' that is defined by the language, when, within Mozambique, most Mozambicans – at least at the time when that [linguistic] 'family' was created – didn't speak Portuguese at all … So what's the place of these Mozambicans in this 'family'? It was thus a project hastily put together, with a clear political intent and at first there was a nervous reaction but then we realised that this project was actually nothing, that it doesn't have any backbone. Yet there's a part of that project that I have some sympathy for. That is, [it would be useful] if these countries [of the CPLP] would agree in relation to global political issues, in times where the world speaks with only one voice. If there would be such a possibility of concertation, another position that unites Brazil, Mozambique, Portugal, Guinea, etc., that would be a good thing, I think. However, the *Lusofonía* I'm interested in is something else. It's an accident.

KVH: … an accident? In what sense?

MC: In the sense of a historical accident. Not in the sense of a disaster! [*laughs*] It's accidental, circumstantial. And it's happening. Unfortunately, if you ask, in Mozambique, who knows the writers of Angola or Cape Verde … we don't know them. We do not know … there is not a real clear intention to know each other.

KVH: I remember something Frank Martinus Arion [the late Curaçaoan writer] said [about the Caribbean]. He said that Creolisation should start with the Caribbean. But his conclusion was disconcerting: what unites us most is ignorance of one another.[2] Is that true for Mozambique too?

2 See Frank Martinus Arion, 'The Great Curassow or The Road to Caribbeanness'. *Callalloo* 21, no. 3 (1998c): 447–452.

MC: It's true. That's what happens to us, too. We have the same language to ignore each other better and I do not see that this is a major official concern to states and governments. [The concern] exists only at the political level, at the institutional level [...]. The books don't circulate, the writers don't circulate. They circulate only when they obey the interests of the commercial market. It's the commercial market that rules. Nowadays publishers decide who will do what, where they will launch their books. The state has completely resigned from this [cultural] area. It's not worth crying and asking CPLP to do something because they won't.

KVH: Technologies are more and more accessible now, including to the poor. This creates the impression that poverty suddenly appears to be resolved; perhaps it is better to say that this reality is also covered in a kind of makeup, in the sense that everyone connects with everyone in real-time, and first of all with the great narrative of Modernity. In spite of the advantages these technologies provide (facilitating communication and compressing distances), do they not also create the (false) illusion that everyone and everything already has the so-called 'first world' within reach, or do they simply prove that the contradiction between modernity and tradition is false? I am also thinking of your scepticism in the face of the global fashion of adopting Americanisms and the language related to technologies, which you refer to in your book *Pensatempos* as a language called *Desenvolvimentês*.[3] What's your position in this regard?

MC: I'm divided. I think there are things here that are contradictory. On the one hand there are now technological processes that put us in sync. For example our use of the Internet: say, on Facebook or on Twitter, I'm in touch with someone in the world, in Afghanistan, Canada, Chile. But does that resolve anything? [...] I do not know if a young man in Canada, simply because of having a friend on Facebook in Afghanistan, knows Afghanistan any better, or has a desire to know another cultural reality. I don't think it's something automatic. It may be a gateway, yes, but what circulates now is more trash than fostering real [cultural] exchange.

KVH: Finally, oral tradition is fundamental in a country like Mozambique. Yet for how long? I recently spoke with Ida Alvarinho,

3 Mia Couto. *Pensatempos – textos de opinião* (Lisbon: Editorial Caminho, 2005).

founder of the Grail [a cultural and literary association for women, based in Maputo], among other things about the current state of orality in Mozambique as well as in the world. I addressed the issue of the loss of the oral word as a means of traditional transference – our ability to tell stories – and one of the factors of this loss would be the omnipresence in our lives of new technologies. We agreed that the latter are not having any particular beneficial effect on people's use of language, especially the younger generations. Is our pessimism justified, or is there reason to be more optimistic?

MC: I'm a pessimist with hope, because I think these processes trigger other things that are unpredictable. For example, the fact that today in the most remote parts of Mozambique, in the Mozambique *profundo* – I do not like to use the word 'deep' because it refers to what we don't know – you have a guy who is talking on the phone with his cousin who is in South Africa and another one in Maputo. This communication network creates something new. It doesn't just work on the surface, as I was saying. [...] There's something else that technology drags with itself. There's an exchange. Something is going on and it is important that these people become producers of information and not just consumers. For example if there is an attack, someone can shoot pictures or videos with their device. We are not dependent any more on a small specialised team of photographers or camera-men, who in turn are dependent on the media outlets of the official producers of information, who have linked the informal side connected to people who produce information [...] And this exchange is not in vain, it produces something new that was not predictable. [...] So I'm not so pessimistic to say that orality lives from those storytellers.

Works cited

Couto, Mia. *Pensatempos – textos de opinião*. Lisbon: Editorial Caminho, 2005.

Notes on Contributors

DAVID BROOKSHAW is an Emeritus Professor at Bristol University, UK. He has a special interest in Lusophone Postcolonial Studies, Comparative Postcolonial Studies, and Literary Translation. He has published widely on Brazilian, Lusophone African, and Luso-Asian literatures. He has organised a number of anthologies, and has translated the fiction of Lusophone African authors including Paulina Chiziane and Mia Couto – most recently Couto's *Mulheres de Cinza*. His translations of Mia Couto's *A Espada e a Azagaia* and selected short stories have just been published.

KAMILA KRAKOWSKA RODRIGUES is a lecturer at the BA Program International Studies at Leiden University, The Netherlands, and an affiliated member of the research centre CESA (Centre for the Studies on Africa, Asia and Latin America) at the University of Lisbon, Portugal. She was awarded the Fernão Mendes Pinto prize for her PhD thesis (Coimbra University, Portugal) on the motif of travel and the formation of national identity in the works by Mário de Andrade and Mia Couto. She co-edited the volume with interviews with Angolan and Mozambican writers *Speaking the Postcolonial Nation* (Peter Lang, 2014) and published several articles on the topic of identity formation in Lusophone literature and cinema.

EWA A. ŁUKASZYK is a Polish comparativist specialising in Lusophone and Mediterranean literatures, and a former professor of the University of Warsaw; currently she lives and works in Leiden. She has authored more than 200 scholarly publications, including seven books in Polish: the latest are *Imperium i nostalgia. „Styl późny" w kulturze portugalskiej* (*Empire and Nostalgia. "Late style" in Portuguese culture*, Warsaw 2015), *Humanistyka, która nadchodzi. W poszukiwaniu kondycji transkulturowej* (*The Coming Humanities. In search of transcultural condition*, Warsaw

2018) and *Mgławica Pessoa. Literatura portugalska od romantyzmu do współczesności* (*Nebula Pessoa. Portuguese literature from Romanticism to the present day*, Wrocław 2019).

IRENE MARQUES is a bilingual writer (English and Portuguese) and Lecturer at Ryerson University in the Department of English where she teaches literature and creative writing. She has also taught at the University of Toronto and York University. Marques holds a PhD in Comparative Literature, a Master's in French and Comparative Literature (University of Toronto) and a Bachelor of Social Work (Ryerson University). Her academic publications include the manuscript *Transnational Discourses on Class, Gender and Cultural Identity* (Purdue University Press, 2011) and numerous articles in international journals or scholarly collectives. She is the author of three poetry collections: *The Circular Incantation: An Exercise in Loss and Findings* (2013, Guernica Editions), *The Perfect Unravelling of the Spirit* (2012, Mawenzi House) and *Wearing Glasses of Water* (2007, Mawenzi House), the short story collection *Habitando na Metáfora do Tempo: Crónicas Desejadas* (2009, Edium Editores) and the novel *My House is a Mansion* (2015, Leaping Lion Books/ York University). Her novel *Uma casa no mundo* (Portuguese) won the Imprensa Nacional Ferreira de Castro Prize (2019) and will be published by Imprensa Nacional (Portugal) in 2020. Her novel *Daria* (English) is scheduled for publication in the fall of 2020 (Inanna Publications, York University, Canada).

CELINA MARTINS is a lecturer at the University of Madeira where she teaches Lusophone and Comparative Literatures. She has a Master's in Comparative Literature at the University of Lisbon (1997) and she was awarded a PhD in Comparative Literature at the University of Madeira in 2004. She has published several articles in a wide range of journals as well as the book *O Entrelaçar das Vozes Mestiças. Análise das Poéticas da Alteridade na ficção de Edouard Glisssant e Mia Couto* (2006). Since 2010, she has been the editor of *Pensardiverso*, a journal of Lusophone Studies at the University of Madeira. Currently, her comparative research focuses on the poetics of Gonçalo M. Tavares, travel writing and utopian studies in contemporary times.

PETER J. MAURITS is postdoctoral fellow at the University Erlangen-Nuremberg. He holds a PhD in comparative literary studies (LMU, Munich), an MA in literary studies (UU, Utrecht), and a BA in Portuguese Literature and Culture (UU, Utrecht). His first book titled *The Mozambican Ghost Story* will be published by Peter Lang. His current research project focuses on African science fiction.

PAULO DE MEDEIROS is Professor of English & Comparative Literature at the University of Warwick where he holds the Chair of Modern & Contemporary World Literatures. Previously he held the Chair of Portuguese Studies at Utrecht University and has taught at several universities in Portugal, Brazil, Spain, and the USA. In 2011–2012 he was appointed Keeley Fellow at Wadham College, Oxford. His research centres on Lusophone narrative, literary and cultural theory with a focus on the interrelations between politics and literature, as well as on postcolonial issues. His most recent book, *O Silêncio das Sereias* (Tinta da China, 2015) on Pessoa's *Book of Disquiet*, was awarded the PEN Portugal prize for best book of essays in 2016. He also edited *Postcolonial Theory and Lusophone Literatures* (Utrecht, 2007) and co-edited a number of journal issues in Portugal as well as in the UK and the USA. One of his current projects is a monograph on Postimperial Europe.

KRISTIAN VAN HAESENDONCK is an Associate Professor and Researcher at the Language and Culture Research Center, University of Sanya (P.R.C.) specialising in comparative Spanish American, postcolonial Caribbean and Lusophone African literatures. He is the author of *Postcolonial Archipelagos: essays on Hispanic Caribbean and Lusophone African Literatures* (Peter Lang, 2017) and *¿Encanto o espanto? Identidad y nación en la novela puertorriqueña actual* (Vervuert-Iberoamericana, 2008), and editor of *Going Caribbean! New Perspectives on Caribbean Literature and Art* (Humus, 2012), and *Caribbeing: Comparing Caribbean Literatures and Cultures* (Rodopi, 2014).

FERNANDA VILAR is a researcher at *MEMOIRS – Children of Empire and European Post-Memories* (ERC Consolidator Grant, no. 648624) at the Centre for Social Studies, University of Coimbra. Her research interests are postcolonial, postmemory, cultural, subaltern and peripheral studies. She is writing a book about the impact of art in the construction of a European citizenship in the peripheries of Lisbon, Paris and Brussels. She was selected by United Nations Academic Impact (UNAI) in 2015 after completing her PhD in African Cultural Studies at Paris Nanterre University. She worked at the European Commission's interpreting service (2016). She received an excellence scholarship for her Master's degree at Ecole Normale Supérieure de Lyon, where she was a lector of Portuguese as a foreign language (2010–2012). She taught Portuguese at the University of Marne la Valée (2012–2013).

RECONFIGURING IDENTITIES IN THE PORTUGUESE-SPEAKING WORLD

Edited by

Paulo de Medeiros and Cláudia Pazos-Alonso

The series publishes studies across the entire spectrum of Lusophone literature, culture and intellectual history, from the Middle Ages to the present day, with particular emphasis on figurations and reconfigurations of identity, broadly understood. It is especially interested in work which interrogates national identity and cultural memory, or which offers fresh insights into Portuguese-speaking cultural and literary traditions, in diverse historical contexts and geographical locations. It is open to a wide variety of approaches and methodologies as well as to interdisciplinary fields: from literary criticism and comparative literature to cultural and gender studies, to film and media studies. It also seeks to encourage critical dialogue among scholarship originating from different continents.

Proposals are welcome for either single-author monographs or edited collections (in English and/or Portuguese). Those interested in contributing to the series should send a detailed project outline to oxford@peterlang.com.

Vol. 1 Ana Margarida Martins: Magic Stones and Flying Snakes: Gender and the 'Postcolonial Exotic' in the Work of Paulina Chiziane and Lídia Jorge.
ISBN 978-3-0343-0828-1. 2012

Vol. 2 Ana Mafalda Leite, Hilary Owen, Rita Chaves, Livia Apa (eds): Narrating the Postcolonial Nation: Mapping Angola and Mozambique.
ISBN 978-3-0343-0891-5. 2014

Vol. 3 Ana Mafalda Leite, Sheila Khan, Jessica Falconi, Kamila Krakowska (eds): Speaking the Postcolonial Nation: Interviews with Writers from Angola and Mozambique.
ISBN 978-3-0343-0890-8. 2014

Vol. 4 Francisco Bethencourt (ed.): Utopia in Portugal, Brazil and Lusophone African Countries.
ISBN 978-3-0343-1871-6. 2015

Vol. 5 Ana Luísa Amaral, Ana Paula Ferreira, Marinela Freitas (eds): New Portuguese Letters to the World: International Reception. ISBN 978-3-0343-1893-8. 2015

Vol. 6 Fernando Beleza and Simon Park (eds): Mário de Sá-Carneiro, A Cosmopolitan Modernist.
ISBN 978-3-0343-1885-3. 2017

Vol. 7 Eleanor K. Jones: Battleground Bodies: Gender and Sexuality in Mozambican Literature.
ISBN 978-1-78707-317-3. 2017

Vol. 8 Maria do Carmo Piçarra and Teresa Castro (eds): (Re)imagining African Independence: Film, Visual Arts and the Fall of the Portuguese Empire.
ISBN 978-1-78707-318-0. 2017

Vol. 9 Maria Manuel Lisboa: A Heaven of Their Own: Heresy and Heterodoxy in Portuguese Literature from the Eighteenth Century to the Present.
ISBN 978-3-0343-1962-1. 2018

Vol. 10 Doris Wieser and Ana Filipa Prata (eds): Cities of the Lusophone World: Literature, Culture and Urban Transformations.
ISBN 978-1-78874-251-1. 2018

Vol. 11 Paulo Pepe and Ana Raquel Fernandes (eds): Beyond Binaries, Sex, Sexualities, and Gender in the Lusophone World.
ISBN 978-1-78707-615-0. 2019

Vol. 12 Ana Mafalda Leite, Jessica Falconi, Kamila Krakowska, Sheila Khan, and Carmen Tindó Secco (eds): Voices, Languages, Discourses: Interpreting the Present and the Memory of Nation in Cape Verde, Guinea-Bissau and São Tomé and Príncipe.
ISBN 978-1-78707-585-6. 2020

Vol. 13 Ana Mafalda Leite, Hilary Owen, Ellen Sapega and Carmen Tindó Secco (eds): Postcolonial Nation and Narrative III: Literature & Cinema. Cape Verde, Guinea-Bissau and São Tomé e Príncipe.
ISBN 978-1-78707-581-8. 2019

Vol. 14 Elena Brugioni, Orlando Grossegesse, and Paulo de Medeiros (eds): A Companion to João Paulo Borges Coelho. ISBN 978-1-78707-986-1. 2020

Vol. 15 Kristian Van Haesendonck (ed.): The Worlds of Mia Couto. ISBN 978-1-78874-594-9. 2020

Lightning Source UK Ltd.
Milton Keynes UK
UKHW022208270121
377781UK00005B/257

9 781788 745949